Theodore Roosevelt (1858-1919), after graduating from Harvard, studied law at Columbia. From 1881-1884 he was a Republican member of the New York state legislature. He served on the U.S. Civil Service Commission (1889-1895), on the New York city police board (1895-1897), and in 1897 became Assistant Secretary of the Navy. During the Spanish-American War, he organized the "Rough Riders," a volunteer regiment which distinguished itself in Cuba. Upon his return from the war, Roosevelt held the office of governor of New York for two years. In 1900 he was elected Vice-President under McKinley, and became our twenty-sixth President the following year, after McKinley's assassination. Roosevelt championed the construction of the Panama Canal and helped to bring about the cessation of the Russo-Japanese War. He sponsored reform legislation and made notable contributions to the cause of conservation during his Presidency. In 1912 he ran again for President, as head of the Progressive or "Bull Moose" party, but was defeated by Wilson.

William E. Leuchtenburg, Professor of History at Columbia University, has taught at New York University, Smith College, Harvard University, and at the Salzburg Seminar for American Studies. He is the author of *Flood Control Politics* and *The Perils of Prosperity, 1914-32* and is a Fellow, 1961-62, of the Center for Advanced Study in the Behavioral Sciences, Stanford, California.

The New Nationalism

The New Nationalism

Theodore Roosevelt

With an Introduction and Notes
by WILLIAM E. LEUCHTENBURG

GLOUCESTER, MASS.
PETER SMITH
1971

Editors' Note

This book is a volume in the Classics in History Series of works in American history. The titles in the series have been chosen primarily from familiar works that are not easily accessible. In some cases we have also chosen to reprint once influential books that still have intrinsic interest or to create fresh collections of essays or letters that now exist only in scattered or expensive editions.

William E. Leuchtenburg
Bernard Wishy

A Note About This Edition

The original edition of *The New Nationalism* was edited by Ernest Hamlin Abbott and published by The Outlook Company in 1910. Abbott put together a portion of the speeches Theodore Roosevelt made in his journey of almost 5,500 miles between August 23 and September 11, 1910. I have followed Abbott's original plan of organization; the material is arranged not chronologically but thematically. The original edition included an introduction by Ernest Hamlin Abbott, an *Outlook* editorial by Lyman Abbott, and an editorial by Theodore Roosevelt, "Criticism of the Courts." I have deleted these, because the Abbott pieces did not seem particularly helpful and because Roosevelt's editorial merely repeated points he had made earlier.

W. E. L.

Table of Contents

xi

TABLE OF CONTENTS

The New Nationalism

Theodore Roosevelt's *The New Nationalism*

As Theodore Roosevelt neared the end of his second term as President in 1908, he took steps to make certain that a man who shared his political outlook would be chosen to succeed him. He found that man in his portly Secretary of War, William Howard Taft. Taft had proved to be a reliable lieutenant and a staunch progressive; sometimes, indeed, he seemed more radical than his chief. To win the nomination for Taft, Roosevelt had to overcome strong opposition from the conservative wing of the party headed by Rhode Island's Senator Nelson Aldrich. The Colonel had good reason to feel content when Taft not only won the nomination but went on to defeat William Jennings Bryan in the 1908 election. If he could not have a third term himself, he felt confident that Taft would carry on the policies he had initiated; it would be almost as though the Colonel himself were still in the White House.

Yet within a few weeks after Roosevelt sailed for Africa, Taft was in deep trouble. He had come to accept much of the viewpoint of the progressives, but, at heart, he was a conservative. He distrusted rebellion, disliked political warfare, and had the temperament not of the leader of a progressive crusade but of a cautious judge. Confronted with problems that Roosevelt had managed to evade, he soon found himself, without knowing quite what had happened, aligned with Aldrich and the Old Guard against his former progressive allies.

It began with the battle for tariff reform in the spring of 1909. Taft was committed to lowering the tariff—he had imbibed William Graham Sumner's free trade views when a student at Yale—but when Aldrich opposed reform, he buckled. The result was the Payne-Aldrich Tariff Act of 1909 with rates substantially as high as the notorious Dingley tariff of a decade before. The progressives were furious because the President had deserted them, but Taft, with his instinct for blunder, made matters still worse by journeying to the progressive heartland of Minnesota and insisting: "I would say without hesitation that this is the best tariff bill that the Republican party has ever passed, and therefore the best tariff bill that has been passed at all."

In the midst of the storm over the tariff debate, a new tempest hit Washington which all but blew Taft out of the White House. Roosevelt, justifiably, felt prouder of his accomplishments in conservation than of any other achievement in the White House. With the aid of his Chief Forester, Gifford Pinchot, and his Secretary of the Interior, James Garfield, he had awakened the nation to the need for conservation. Roosevelt had been dismayed when Taft, after indicating he would reappoint Garfield, had chosen instead the former mayor of Seattle and later Commissioner of the Land Office, Richard Achilles Ballinger. Pinchot, suspicious of Ballinger from the beginning, engaged in a running war with the new Secretary from the moment he took office. When Louis Glavis of the Land Office came to Pinchot with evidence that Ballinger was privy to a conspiracy of a Morgan-Guggenheim syndicate to acquire government coal lands in Alaska, Pinchot rushed to Taft with the story. Taft responded by sustaining Ballinger and firing Glavis.

Yet Taft still hoped to avoid an open break with Pinchot. Even though he thought him a "fanatic," he sought to hold on to the Forester, because he did not want it to appear that he had repudiated Roosevelt's policies. But the hot-tempered Pinchot forced his hand. When Pinchot let it be known that he had been feeding confidential information from government files to the press, Taft had no choice but to remove him from office in January 1910. Now the fat was in the fire. It later became clear that Ballinger, while no friend of conservation, was not actually implicated in any conspiracy, and Taft was to go on to make substantial contributions to conservation. But the country, which could not follow the involved machinations of the Alaskan claims, grasped the chief point: that Taft had removed from office one of Teddy Roosevelt's closest associates, and the leading advocate of forest conservation in America, over a dispute in which the President appeared to be siding with Morgan and Guggenheim.

By March 1910, the division between Taft and the insurgents—as the rebellious progressives came to be called—had grown into open warfare. Taft had moved completely into the camp of the conservatives. Some months later, he would write Aldrich: "I long for your presence. I feel about as Scott said of Rhoderick Dhu—a blast upon your bugle horn were worth a thousand men." Taft not only took the conservative view on legislative issues, but sought to destroy the insurgents politically. He gave patronage to their enemies, and laid plans with Aldrich and Speaker "Uncle Joe" Cannon to use the prestige of the White House to defeat the insurgents in the Republican primaries that spring.

Roosevelt viewed all these developments with increasing concern, but he did his best to withhold judgment. He had gone to Africa in part to give Taft a chance to prove himself. He was not a factionalist, and he did not want to hurt the Republican Party. A deep-dyed Republican, he flinched from splitting the party and turning the country over to the Democrats, that party of disunion, vacillation, and bad morals. Moreover, he knew that many would view any criticism of Taft by the former president as an act of disloyalty or even the petulance of a power-hungry man who could not stand to see another in his place. Yet he was aggrieved by Taft's decision to pass over Roosevelt men in his cabinet choices and piqued by reports of incivilities to members of his family by members of Taft's family. Nor was it easy to ignore the heightened tempo of criticism of the president in early 1910. "Taft," an Indianapolis publisher wrote Roosevelt in March, "is a damn, pig-headed blunderer."

Yet not until April 1910, when Gifford Pinchot crossed the ocean to see him, did the insurgent anger at Taft finally make its mark. Roosevelt conferred for two hours with Pinchot in a woods near Porto Maurizio. The Forester carried heavy ammunition—not only his own account of the Ballinger affair but bitter anti-Taft missiles from good friends of the Colonel like Senator Albert Beveridge of Indiana, Senator Jonathan Dolliver of Iowa, and the Kansas editor, William Allen White. Never thereafter was Roosevelt able to place his trust in Taft. Early in May, he wrote his friend Senator Henry Cabot Lodge, a leader of the conservatives: "For a year after Taft took office, for a year and a quarter after he had been elected, I would not let myself think ill of anything he did. I finally had to admit that he had gone wrong on certain points; and I then also had to admit to myself that deep down underneath I had all along known he was wrong, on points as to which I had tried to deceive myself, by loudly proclaiming to myself, that he was right."

All that spring Republican leaders awaited anxiously Roosevelt's return. The insurgents, convinced that their only hope lay in nominating Roosevelt rather than Taft in 1912, raised the cry: "Back from Elba!" They hoped the Colonel would immediately join forces with them in their war with Taft. On the other hand, conservative friends like Lodge urged him to return to reunite the Republican party behind Taft. Roosevelt was in a quandary. He did not want to join the insurgents, because he wished to do nothing to divide the party further, and he still hoped that Taft would "retrieve himself." At the same time, he wrote Lodge that he refused to take responsibility for the failure of the "Taft-Aldrich-Cannon regime" to appreciate the needs of the country.

Roosevelt insisted he would not be used by cynical Republican

4

politicians who wanted him only for the purpose of corralling progressive support on Election Day and then would ignore him and his ideas. He felt that Taft had broken his pledge to follow a progressive course, and that, in so doing, he was destroying the Republican party. Contemptuous of the Democrats and proud of the strength of the party he had turned over to Taft in March 1909, he was disgusted by the manner in which in a few months Taft had undone his work and given the Democrats their best opportunity in twenty years. The plight of the Republican party, and the recognition that he was caught in an impossible situation plunged him into one of his periodic moods of pessimism. "Ugh! I do dread getting back to America, and having to plunge into this cauldron of politics," he wrote. "Our own party leaders do not realize that I was able to hold the Republican party in power only because I insisted on a steady advance, and dragged them along with me."

"If there is to be a great crowd, do arrange so that the whole crowd has a chance to see me and that there is as little disappointment as possible," Roosevelt wrote a friend in the spring of 1910. On June 18, 1910, after more than a year abroad hunting African lions and lecturing European monarchs, the Colonel returned home to a monster reception in New York Harbor. Reporters were alerted to watch even the smallest indication of whom Roosevelt would support; much was made of the fact that one of Roosevelt's first acts after he landed was to call out "Hello Gifford." Within ten days after his arrival, both Gifford Pinchot and Senator Robert LaFollette of Wisconsin, the leader of the Senate insurgents, had called on him at Oyster Bay.

Yet Roosevelt still sought to avert a split in the party. "I shall keep my mind as open as I keep my mouth shut," he promised. If the Colonel's sympathies lay with the insurgents, a hard-headed appreciation of the cold political realities led him to pursue a course of moderation. He cautioned Gifford Pinchot that while he shared keenly his disappointment in Taft, it was important to keep in mind that in another two years it would probably be "necessary to

renominate Taft, and eminently desirable to re-elect him over any-
one whom there is the least likelihood of the Democrats naming."
Taft, Roosevelt told Pinchot, might even yet become "a perfectly
respectable President." Moreover, he warned that he himself would
not be nominated in 1912, if the nomination did not go to Taft,
"unless everybody believed that the ship was sinking and thought
it a good thing to have me aboard her when she went down."

Roosevelt turned aside all pleas that he choose sides. He reasoned
that, if he joined either faction, he would lose all favor with the
other group. Moreover, he feared that if he supported the insurgents, he would drive them to take such radical positions that they
would alienate much of the country. On August 17, Roosevelt com-
plained to Lodge that Taft was associated in the public mind with
men like Aldrich and Cannon, and that "we have had no National
leadership of any real kind since election day 1908." Yet he conceded that the anti-Taft leadership had "tended to fall exclusively
into the hands of narrow fanatics, wild visionaries and self-seeking
demagogues." Instead of choosing sides, he resolved to tour the
country in an attempt to heal party wounds and effect a new har-
many in the G.O.P. Yet he had no illusions. He knew he would
probably wind up not only having failed in his mission but having
incurred the enmity of both factions.

By the summer of 1910, the party seemed past reuniting. Taft
was seeking to take the political lives of the insurgents, and the
rebels were handing him a bad beating. In June, the Iowa insurgents won a smashing victory in the primaries; the voters returned
every incumbent progressive Congressman and ousted two conservative Representatives. In midsummer, Kansas voters turned out four
of six Old Guard Congressmen, although the state had been told
that the election would be taken as a vote of confidence or no-
confidence in President Taft. In mid-August, Hiram Johnson, tour-
ing California in his "red devil" automobile, waving his hands in

the T. R. manner, and shouting "Bully!" as often as he could, won a smashing victory over the Taft Republicans.

When Roosevelt headed west in late August, he thought that his first duty was to assure the progressives that he had not deserted them, and that he was not responsible for the actions of the man he had foisted upon them. As early as May, he had written Lodge from Norway: "Remember that there are a great multitude of men inclined to forgive me on the ground that I was deceived, as they were, but who would not forgive me if I now went ahead, as they would regard it, to continue the deception."

Roosevelt lost no time in redeeming himself in the eyes of the insurgents. In Denver, at the very beginning of his tour, he hurled a heavy artillery barrage at the most awesome of the foes of progressives, the courts. Roosevelt charged that the courts had created a borderland where neither federal nor state governments could exercise control of business corporations. The bench had handed down decisions "arbitrarily and irresponsibly limiting the power of the people." Before the newspapers carrying denunciations by conservative editors of his Denver speeches were out on the streets, the Colonel was headed toward Kansas, the very center of the rebellion against Taft. Even after midnight, crowds in small Kansas towns stood in a relentless downpour at country depots to catch a glimpse of Roosevelt's train headed toward Osawatomie. Here at Osawatomie, a town whose very name suggested bloody rebellion, Roosevelt set forth the doctrines of the New Nationalism.

The insurgents were overjoyed. Roosevelt, it seemed, had joined them at last. Kansans interpreted his speech not only as a specific endorsement of the insurgent platform adopted the day before, but as a bold challenge to Taft for the 1912 Republican nomination. On the way home from Osawatomie, Kansas insurgents, celebrating in the aisles of the train, passed out the new slogan: "Roosevelt for 1912." In Nebraska, progressives called a conference to organize a Roosevelt-Dolliver slate for 1912.

The conservatives were horrified by Roosevelt's doctrines and by the implications for 1912. The *Brooklyn Eagle* denounced Roosevelt's observations on the courts in Denver as "inexcusable"; the Baltimore *Sun* accused him of aping Bryan; and the *Denver Republican* called the speech a more violent statement than Calhoun's doctrine of nullification. But the choicest invective was saved for the Osawatomie speech. *Harper's Weekly* called Roosevelt "a virtual traitor"; the *World* denounced the New Nationalism as "an outburst of Marxian madness," and critics compared the former President to Kaiser Wilhelm, Julius Caesar, Catiline, and Porfirio Diaz. As he wrote his son Ted on September 21: "New York for the last four weeks has been nearly insane over me, feeling that I have become well-nigh an anarchist—or a communist, which they consider an identical term."

Both the insurgents and the conservatives misunderstood Roosevelt. He had not joined sides and he had no specific ambitions for 1912. When a luncheon group in Kansas City sang a song which called the Colonel an "insurgent through and through," he replied pointedly that it would be better to call him a "progressive." At Sioux City, he praised Taft for recommending a tariff commission, and in Syracuse he sought to placate the conservatives on his stand on the courts. He still held to his original position, he wrote Lodge four days later, but "I had no business to take that position in the fashion I did." He conceded that it was "a blunder of some gravity" not to have explained his position more carefully in Denver. Before the end of the campaign, the West was incensed by Roosevelt's concessions to Taft and the conservatives. His tour had ended just as badly as he had feared it would. Both factions were displeased, and the party was so badly rent that the split of 1912 was all but inevitable. Instead of uniting the party, Roosevelt had only divided it more deeply.

Much of the confusion about Roosevelt's position came from a misguided attempt to classify him either as a progressive or a business-oriented conservative when Roosevelt, in fact, was neither.

He approached the political problems of the day with quite different assumptions from the humanitarian reformer, committed to advancing the interests of the underprivileged, or from the business-minded conservative, opposed to any change that might jeopardize the interests of the propertied classes.

Roosevelt believed that the country faced the most serious crisis since the eve of the Civil War. Over and over again in his letters in 1910, he returned to the analogy between the division in the Republican party and the troubles which had destroyed the pre-war Whigs. As the occasion to introduce the New Nationalism, he chose the dedication ceremonies of John Brown's battlefield at Osawatomie. He held up to both factions the ideal of Abraham Lincoln, the Lincoln who was the saint of American nationalism, the man who had risked bloody civil strife to preserve the nation, and who, on the eve of triumph in a war to unite the nation, had been martyred on Good Friday. Americans of Roosevelt's generation came close to transforming the Lincoln legend into a secular cult; the California progressive leader William Kent's only religious affiliation was with the Abraham Lincoln Center of Chicago.

Roosevelt traced the source of the new crisis facing the country to the fact that men lacked a sense of national unity. The nation was still much too parochial in its outlook, too sectionally-minded in its attitude toward American politics, too provincial in its view of the world. More serious even than this parochialism were the actions of two warring classes, capital and labor, both of which pursued their private advantages heedless of the national interest. Roosevelt had the deep contempt of the patrician for the greedy businessman who lacked even a primitive sense of justice. He felt at the same time a horror of mob violence; he saw in each new labor leader, in each new tribune of the people, a potential Robespierre. Throughout his western trip, he warned that the Scylla of demagogism was as much to be dreaded as the Charybdis of conservatism; the reckless agitator and the unscrupulous reactionary both stood "on the same plane of obnoxiousness."

9

The factions which threatened to divide the nation were the very factions whose extreme members threatened to disrupt the Republican party, Roosevelt believed. The conservatives who fawned on business, he wrote Lodge in mid-September, were "really the heirs of the cotton Whigs, and not of the Republicanism of Lincoln." On the other hand, the radical wing of the insurgents posed the same threat to sane politics that John Brown once had. A few weeks before he went to Osawatomie, he explained: "At the moment, I am endeavoring to prevent the John Browns among the insurgents getting themselves in a position from which the Abraham Lincolns cannot extricate them." In December after the state campaigns had been fought and lost to the Democrats, a weary and melancholy Roosevelt made one more attempt to explain his position: "I wish to be radical, as Lincoln was radical compared to Buchanan and Fillmore, and conservative as he was conservative compared to Wendell Phillips and John Brown."

As the Lincoln who would reunite a fragmented nation, Roosevelt insisted that the national interest was prior to any individual right. At Osawatomie, he had made the bold assertion: "The man who wrongly holds that every human right is secondary to his profit must now give way to the advocate of human welfare, who rightly maintains that every man holds his property subject to the general right of the community to regulate its use to whatever degree the public welfare may require it." The rights of the community, greater than any individual rights, would best be advanced, Roosevelt argued, by a powerful central government. Since business had been nationalized, states and localities were no longer able to cope with "lawbreakers of great wealth"; only the federal government could do so. It should have power to complete its tasks, unfettered by the casuistries of judges who would shackle it. The hope of the people lay not in the courts but in a vigorous Chief Executive who would be "the steward of the public welfare."

Roosevelt had a peculiarly European concern with the health of the state. The great menace to the health of the nation, Roosevelt believed, lay in the utilitarianism of a business civilization, insensible to national honor, and that popular pursuit of ease which placed rights above duties, pleasures above the national interest. A people unwilling to sacrifice for the good of the state was a decadent people; the New Nationalism would seek, by teaching and by action, to reinvigorate American society. "Social efficiency," Roosevelt thought, derived from "love of order, ability to fight well and breed well, capacity to subordinate the interests of the individual to the interests of the community."

Many of Roosevelt's contemporaries believed that Roosevelt had drawn the doctrines of the New Nationalism directly from the American political philosopher, Herbert Croly. In the 1912 campaign, for example, the *American Magazine* described Croly as "the man from whom Colonel Roosevelt got his 'New Nationalism.'" Roosevelt had had his attention called to Croly's *The Promise of American Life,* published in 1909, by both Learned Hand and Henry Cabot Lodge, not in Africa, as is sometimes said, but on his tour of Europe as he headed home for America. Sometime in the late spring or early summer of 1910, Roosevelt read Croly's study. In late July, at a time when the Colonel was preparing his speeches for his western tour, he wrote Croly: "I do not know when I have read a book which I felt profited me as much as your book on American life." Roosevelt added: "I shall use your ideas freely in speeches I intend to make."

Such direct evidence of the influence of a writer on a public man is more than most historians ever hope to find, and it is little wonder that they have made so much of the impact of Croly on Roosevelt. They have not only suggested that he influenced the New Nationalism but have gone still further to argue that Croly converted Roosevelt from the conservatism of his White House years to the advanced progressivism of the Bull Moose campaign of 1912. Such a view of Croly's influence arises from the mistaken conviction that Roosevelt as President was a fraud, a conservative masquerading as a reformer. Since no one could deny that the Colonel made a radical appeal in 1912, historians who conceive of Roosevelt as a pseudo-progressive as president have felt compelled to explain the "change" in Roosevelt and to attribute it to some external agent.

The notion that the Colonel changed the views of a lifetime as the result of reading one book betrays a wistful faith in the power of the pen, but little else. There is scarcely a theme or a recommendation of the New Nationalism which Roosevelt had not already enunciated before Croly wrote his book. In three messages to Congress in 1907 and 1908, Roosevelt had spelled out almost the entire program of the New Nationalism: federal regulation of business, legislation to benefit labor, the inheritance and income taxes, and instrumentalities like postal savings banks. He had accused individual business leaders of "rottenness," of "flagrant dishonesty," and of "bitter and unscrupulous craft." He had urged that workers be guaranteed "a larger share of the wealth." He had assaulted the judiciary, and especially the federal courts, and had suggested that some judges were "incompetent." Well before 1907, in private letters and in some public acts, he had foreshadowed the main outlines of New Nationalist thought: nationalism, love of order, alarm at both corporation and union power, fear of revolution, distrust of the Jeffersonian tradition of reform, faith in a strong state and a powerful Chief Executive—the list could be extended to embrace every important tenet of the New Nationalism.

This is not to say Croly had no importance at all. The book could hardly have helped but have a great appeal to Roosevelt not only because it mirrored his own thinking but also because the Colonel was the hero of the book. It probably prodded Roosevelt to clarify his thoughts in the summer of 1910, and he may even, as many writers have suggested, have taken the very phrase "New Nationalism" from Croly, although this seems unlikely. Some of the words Roosevelt spoke at Osawatomie seemed to be a direct response to Croly's urging that he carry his thinking to its logical conclusion. But *The Promise of American Life* is less important for the impact Croly had on Roosevelt than as evidence of the impact Roosevelt had on Croly. In Croly's work, we can find a more systematic statement of Roosevelt's New Nationalism than Roosevelt himself ever found time to set down, and for this reason it commands our attention.

The central argument of *The Promise of American Life* rests on the premise that the ills of American society can be traced to the persistence of Jeffersonian thinking. Croly believed that Jefferson, a man of "intellectual superficiality and insincerity," had started the country off on the wrong foot. Jefferson's "cant" about equal rights for all and special privileges for none had licensed greed and the pursuit of self-interest without regard to the national interest. Instead of seeking to create and sustain fluid elites, Jefferson had prattled about the equality of all men. By his suspicion of concentrated power, he had obscured the need for a strong central government which would direct the fortunes of the nation with a coherent sense of national purpose.

The familiar cliché about Croly is that he favored the achievement of Jeffersonian ends by Hamiltonian means. To say this is to misunderstand Croly altogether. Jefferson is the villain of *The Promise of American Life,* and Croly condemns Jeffersonian ends as well as Jeffersonian means. A truckler to the masses, Jefferson, Croly declared, wanted "a government of and by the people," when he should have sought "a government for the people by popular but responsible leaders." The gross error of Jeffersonianism was that it supposed that "the people were to guide their leaders, not their leaders the people."

Jefferson's "fatal policy of drift," Croly argued, fixed the course of American history for the next century. Jackson perpetuated the Jeffersonian errors, especially the equal rights fetishism and the suspicion of the expert. In the Jacksonian era, "Americans of intelligence" were subjected to "social equalitarianism." For a time, under Lincoln, when all of the resources of the nation were mobilized to wipe out slavery, the country did achieve a sense of national purpose. Lincoln rallied the nation to a sense of its responsibilities by refusing to allow local and individual rights to stand in his way; the war itself "began to emancipate the American national idea from an obscurantist individualism and provincialism." Unhappily, as soon as the war ended, the country slipped back into an aimless policy of drift.

In the years since the Civil War, Croly continued, the industrialization of the country had destroyed the homogeneous society of the early republic. Jefferson's ideas had been mischievous even then, but in the world of the early twentieth century, they were downright dangerous. The doctrine of equal rights had resulted, paradoxically, in the concentration of wealth and power in the hands of a few. The founding fathers had imagined neither such concentration of financial power nor the growth of special interests like labor unions; to cope with them, America needed to develop both a body of opinion and instrumentalities strong enough to discipline both in the national interest. To replace the instinctive homogeneity of 1800, the nation had to reconstruct a new "democratic social ideal." But every attempt to achieve "a national purpose" broke against the fatalistic faith in progress, the irresponsible optimism of a people who thought that, despite the revolutionary changes in American society, they could afford to drift along without taking conscious action in pursuit of a national ideal.

To be sure, there had been countless efforts at reform, Croly conceded, but the reform movement had been cursed by the old Jeffersonian emphases. The reformer's faith in individualism and equal rights had led him to reject the need for a stratified society and to embrace the folly of trust busting. A reformer like Bryan who was a Democrat started out with a fatal handicap, for his party distrusted the concentration of power in the state. Moreover, Bryan's idealization of the common man and his suspicion of the exceptional man meant that he stood for "the sacrifice of the individual to the popular average; and the perpetuation of such a sacrifice would mean ultimate democratic degeneration." An even greater danger came from Jacobins like William Randolph Hearst who abused businessmen by holding them up to public scorn instead of recognizing that politics must be grounded in "mutual confidence and fair dealing."

Fortunately, Croly wrote, there was one reformer "whose work has tended to give reform the dignity of a constructive mission": Theodore Roosevelt. Roosevelt's strength arose from the fact that he was even more a nationalist than a reformer. He had nationalized the reform movement by reviving "the Hamiltonian ideal of constructive national legislation," while at the same time being, as Hamilton was not, a democrat. Roosevelt, with his sense of the national interest, his faith in a strong state, and his willingness to give power to exceptional men, had served "to emancipate American democracy from its Jeffersonian bondage." He had given the Republican party, which had slipped back into the ineffectiveness of the old Whig party, some sense of "its historic mission."

But Roosevelt was not yet the perfect reformer, Croly observed, for he was not yet the perfect nationalist. He continued, at times, to talk the language of Jeffersonianism. What was "the square deal" but an unhappy revival of the assumptions of equal rights, including the demagogic assumption that businessmen had been acting like dishonest sharpers? Fortunately, Roosevelt was building better than he knew or would admit. He was, in fact, a thoroughgoing nationalist whose actions pointed him toward a complete break with the Jeffersonian tradition. Nevertheless, Croly concluded, the danger remained that, so long as Roosevelt refused to acknowledge this fact, the reform movement with which he was associated might go astray.

In his western tour in 1910, Roosevelt did not altogether come to terms with Croly's strictures. Yet he did take another step along the path he had been moving away from the old reform tradition which emphasized natural rights, egalitarianism, and the limited state. His 1910 speeches anticipated the Progressive Party program of 1912. That year, in contrast to Woodrow Wilson's "New Freedom," with its emphasis on a return to the maxims of a nineteenth-century society, Roosevelt would advocate a great augmentation of power of the federal government. In 1912, he would say more than he had in 1910 about permitting the trusts to develop, rather than breaking them up; readers of *The New Nationalism* are often astonished to find that there is only a single passage about the trusts, that it is not at all a book about trusts. In 1912, too, he would come out for welfare measures that he had not yet come to advocate in 1910. But all the main features of the Bull Moose program had been sketched in 1910.

The New Nationalism would be the most fruitful doctrine of the Progressive era, for it stated the underlying assumptions of much of what was later to be known as the Welfare State. Liberated from the fear of centralized authority, political leaders could, for the first time, use the powers of the federal government to make an industrial society more humane. Freed from the unrealistic assumption that every worker was a potential entrepreneur, the government began to take steps to recognize rights of workingmen which previously had been denied. No longer bound by the view that the state should be, at most, an umpire, government officials could embark on bold new programs of regional planning, slum clearance, and public power development.

Yet the New Nationalism too raised disturbing questions about the relation of progressive values to the omnicompetent state. Roosevelt minimized the danger in unrestrained exercise of power by the Executive, yet he himself had demonstrated on many occasions the perils of the lawless use of power by a president who confused his own obsessions with the "national interest." He saw little danger in the cartelization of American society, yet the concentration of decision-making in the hands of a few government and corporation leaders raised a decided threat to individual liberties, quite apart from the question of whether corporations so powerful would not soon control the state.

Even more doubtful was the conception of Roosevelt and Croly that man should find fulfillment in service to the state, the nation-state which Croly insisted had an individuality of its own. Although Croly saw an important role for voluntaristic organization, he based most of his hopes on the state. The Promise of American Life was to be fulfilled not by a maximum grant of freedom, or by the abundant satisfaction of wants, "but by a large measure of individual subordination and self-denial . . . to the fulfillment of a national purpose." Instead of speaking simply for a collectivity of individuals, the New Nationalists' state, Croly explained, would act for "the nation of yesterday and tomorrow, organized for its national historical mission." Both leaders and people would subordinate their desires to "a morally authoritative Sovereign will."

Much as in Bismarck's Germany, Roosevelt and many of the progressives who followed him used as their touchstone the health of the state and its mystical sense of national mission. The same state which promised new social benefits could also embark on nationalistic wars and crush out dissent, also in the name of patriotic ideals. The New Nationalism, Croly explained, was to be "unscrupulously" nationalistic. In 1916, the Progressive Party, which helped give birth to the idea of a positive state dedicated to social welfare, would be destroyed in the name of a positive state dedicated to chauvinism and military preparedness. In the end, as many had always feared, Roosevelt's nationalism ran deeper than his progressivism.

William E. Leuchtenburg

PART ONE

The New Nationalism

The New Nationalism

Speech at Osawatomie
31 AUGUST 1910

We come here to-day to commemorate one of the epoch-making events of the long struggle for the rights of man—the long struggle for the uplift of humanity.[1] Our country—this great republic—means nothing unless it means the triumph of a real democracy, the triumph of popular government, and, in the long run, of an economic system under which each man shall be guaranteed the opportunity to show the best that there is in him. That is why the history of America is now the central feature of the history of the world; for the world has set its face hopefully toward our democracy; and, O my fellow citizens, each one of you carries on your shoulders not only the burden of doing well for the sake of your own country, but the burden of doing well and of seeing that this nation does well for the sake of mankind.

There have been two great crises in our country's history:

[1] The occasion for Roosevelt's speech was the dedication as a state park of the field at Osawatomie where John Brown had fought the Missouri raiders fifty-four years before. Roosevelt spoke in a grove on the battlefield to a dense crowd. Many in his audience had ridden all night in a drenching rain to hear him. The Kansas insurgents, fresh from the Topeka convention, had attached their train to Roosevelt's at Osage City, and travelled to Osawatomie with him. On the platform with Roosevelt, in addition to Gifford Pinchot and James R. Garfield, sat the leaders of the Kansas insurgency: Governor William R. Stubbs, Senator Joseph L. Bristow, Representative Edmund H. Madison, and the Emporia editor, William Allen White.

first, when it was formed, and then, again, when it was perpetuated; and, in the second of these great crises—in the time of stress and strain which culminated in the Civil War, on the outcome of which depended the justification of what had been done earlier, you men of the Grand Army, you men who fought through the Civil War, not only did you justify your generation, not only did you render life worth living for our generation, but you justified the wisdom of Washington and Washington's colleagues. If this republic had been founded by them only to be split asunder into fragments when the strain came, then the judgment of the world would have been that Washington's work was not worth doing. It was you who crowned Washington's work, as you carried to achievement the high purpose of Abraham Lincoln.

Now, with this second period of our history the name of John Brown will be forever associated; and Kansas was the theater upon which the first act of the second of our great national life dramas was played. It was the result of the struggle in Kansas which determined that our country should be in deed as well as in name devoted to both union and freedom; that the great experiment of democratic government on a national scale should succeed and not fail. In name we had the Declaration of Independence in 1776; but we gave the lie by our acts to the words of the Declaration of Independence until 1865; and words count for nothing except in so far as they represent acts. This is true everywhere; but, O my friends, it should be truest of all in political life. A broken promise is bad enough in private life. It is worse in the field of politics. No man is worth his salt in public life who makes on the stump a pledge which he does not keep after election; and, if he makes such a pledge and does not keep it, hunt him out of public life.[2] I care for the great deeds of the past chiefly as spurs to drive

[2] Roosevelt interpolated these words into the original version of his speech. The Kansas crowd greeted them with a tremendous shout. They were taken as an attack on President Taft who had pledged in 1908 to lower the tariff but had capitulated to Republican protectionists who had passed the high Payne-Aldrich tariff in 1909.

us onward in the present. I speak of the men of the past partly
that they may be honored by our praise of them, but more that
they may serve as examples for the future.

It was a heroic struggle; and, as is inevitable with all such
struggles, it had also a dark and terrible side. Very much was
done of good, and much also of evil; and, as was inevitable in
such a period of revolution, often the same man did both good
and evil. For our great good fortune as a nation, we, the people of
the United States as a whole, can now afford to forget the evil,
or, at least, to remember it without bitterness, and to fix our eyes
with pride only on the good that was accomplished. Even in
ordinary times there are very few of us who do not see the problems of life as through a glass, darkly; and when the glass is
clouded by the murk of furious popular passion, the vision of
the best and the bravest is dimmed. Looking back, we are all of
us now able to do justice to the valor and the disinterestedness and
the love of the right, as to each it was given to see the right,
shown both by the men of the North and the men of the South
in that contest which was finally decided by the attitude of the
West. We can admire the heroic valor, the sincerity, the self-de-
votion shown alike by the men who wore the blue and the men
who wore the gray; and our sadness that such men should have
had to fight one another is tempered by the glad knowledge that
ever hereafter their descendants shall be found fighting side by
side, struggling in peace as well as in war for the uplift of their
common country, all alike resolute to raise to the highest pitch of
honor and usefulness the nation to which they all belong. As for
the veterans of the Grand Army of the Republic, they deserve
honor and recognition such as is paid to no other citizens of the
republic; for to them the republic owes its all; for to them it
owes its very existence. It is because of what you and your comrades
did in the dark years that we of to-day walk, each of us, head
erect, and proud that we belong, not to one of a dozen little

squabbling contemptible commonwealths, but to the mightiest nation upon which the sun shines.

I do not speak of this struggle of the past merely from the historic standpoint. Our interest is primarily in the application to-day of the lessons taught by the contest of half a century ago. It is of little use for us to pay lip loyalty to the mighty men of the past unless we sincerely endeavor to apply to the problems of the present precisely the qualities which in other crises enabled the men of that day to meet those crises. It is half melancholy and half amusing to see the way in which well-meaning people gather to do honor to the men who, in company with John Brown, and under the lead of Abraham Lincoln, faced and solved the great problems of the nineteenth century, while, at the same time, these same good people nervously shrink from, or frantically denounce, those who are trying to meet the problems of the twentieth century in the spirit which was accountable for the successful solution of the problems of Lincoln's time.

Of that generation of men to whom we owe so much, the man to whom we owe most is, of course, Lincoln. Part of our debt to him is because he forecast our present struggle and saw the way out. He said:—

I hold that while man exists it is his duty to improve not only his own condition, but to assist in ameliorating mankind.

And again:—

Labor is prior to, and independent of, capital. Capital is only the fruit of labor, and could never have existed if labor had not first existed. Labor is the superior of capital, and deserves much the higher consideration.

If that remark was original with me, I should be even more strongly denounced as a communist agitator than I shall be anyhow. It is Lincoln's. I am only quoting it; and that is one side;

24

that is the side the capitalist should hear. Now, let the workingman hear his side.

> Capital has its rights, which are as worthy of protection as any other
> rights. . . . Nor should this lead to a war upon the owners of prop-
> erty. Property is the fruit of labor; . . . property is desirable; is a
> positive good in the world.

And then comes a thoroughly Lincolnlike sentence:—

> Let not him who is houseless pull down the house of another, but
> let him work diligently and build one for himself, thus by example
> assuring that his own shall be safe from violence when built.

It seems to me that, in these words, Lincoln took substantially
the attitude that we ought to take; he showed the proper sense
of proportion in his relative estimates of capital and labor, of
human rights and property rights. Above all, in this speech, as
in many others, he taught a lesson in wise kindliness and charity;
an indispensable lesson to us of to-day. But this wise kindliness
and charity never weakened his arm or numbed his heart. We
cannot afford weakly to blind ourselves to the actual conflict which
faces us to-day. The issue is joined, and we must fight or fail.

In every wise struggle for human betterment one of the main
objects, and often the only object, has been to achieve in large
measure equality of opportunity. In the struggle for this great end,
nations rise from barbarism to civilization, and through it people
press forward from one stage of enlightenment to the next. One
of the chief factors in progress is the destruction of special privilege.
The essence of any struggle for healthy liberty has always been,
and must always be, to take from some one man or class of men
the right to enjoy power, or wealth, or position, or immunity,
which has not been earned by service to his or their fellows. That
is what you fought for in the Civil War, and that is what we
strive for now.

At many stages in the advance of humanity, this conflict between the men who possess more than they have earned and the men who have earned more than they possess is the central condition of progress. In our day it appears as the struggle of free men to gain and hold the right of self-government as against the special interests, who twist the methods of free government into machinery for defeating the popular will. At every stage, and under all circumstances, the essence of the struggle is to equalize opportunity, destroy privilege, and give to the life and citizenship of every individual the highest possible value both to himself and to the commonwealth. That is nothing new. All I ask in civil life is what you fought for in the Civil War. I ask that civil life be carried on according to the spirit in which the army was carried on. You never get perfect justice, but the effort in handling the army was to bring to the front the men who could do the job. Nobody grudged promotion to Grant, or Sherman, or Thomas, or Sheridan, because they earned it. The only complaint was when a man got promotion which he did not earn.

Practical equality of opportunity for all citizens, when we achieve it, will have two great results. First, every man will have a fair chance to make of himself all that in him lies; to reach the highest point to which his capacities, unassisted by special privilege of his own and unhampered by the special privilege of others, can carry him, and to get for himself and his family substantially what he has earned. Second, equality of opportunity means that the commonwealth will get from every citizen the highest service of which he is capable. No man who carries the burden of the special privileges of another can give to the commonwealth that service to which it is fairly entitled.

I stand for the square deal. But when I say that I am for the square deal, I mean not merely that I stand for fair play under the present rules of the game, but that I stand for having those rules changed so as to work for a more substantial equality of opportunity and of reward for equally good service. One word of warning, which, I think, is hardly necessary in Kansas. When I say I want a square deal for the poor man, I do not mean that I want a square deal for the man who remains poor because he has not the energy to work for himself. If a man who has had a chance will not make good, then he has got to quit. And you men of the Grand Army, you want justice for the brave man who fought, and punishment for the coward who shirked his work. Is not that so?

Now, this means that our government, national and state, must be freed from the sinister influence or control of special interests. Exactly as the special interests of cotton and slavery threatened our political integrity before the Civil War, so now the great special business interests too often control and corrupt the men and methods of government for their own profit. We must drive the special interests out of politics. That is one of our tasks to-day. Every special interest is entitled to justice—full, fair, and complete, —and, now, mind you, if there were any attempt by mob violence to plunder and work harm to the special interest, whatever it may be, that I most dislike, and the wealthy man, whomsoever he may be, for whom I have the greatest contempt, I would fight for him, and you would if you were worth your salt. He should have justice. For every special interest is entitled to justice, but not one is entitled to a vote in Congress, to a voice on the bench, or to representation in any public office. The Constitution guarantees protection to property, and we must make that promise good. But it does not give the right of suffrage to any corporation.

The true friend of property, the true conservative, is he who insists that property shall be the servant and not the master of the commonwealth; who insists that the creature of man's making shall be the servant and not the master of the man who made it. The citizens of the United States must effectively control the mighty commercial forces which they have themselves called into being.

There can be no effective control of corporations while their political activity remains. To put an end to it will be neither a short nor an easy task, but it can be done.

We must have complete and effective publicity of corporate affairs, so that the people may know beyond peradventure whether the corporations obey the law and whether their management entitles them to the confidence of the public. It is necessary that laws should be passed to prohibit the use of corporate funds directly or indirectly for political purposes; it is still more necessary that such laws should be thoroughly enforced. Corporate expenditures for political purposes, and especially such expenditures by public service corporations, have supplied one of the principal sources of corruption in our political affairs.

It has become entirely clear that we must have government supervision of the capitalization, not only of public service corporations, including, particularly, railways, but of all corporations doing an interstate business. I do not wish to see the nation forced into the ownership of the railways if it can possibly be avoided, and the only alternative is thoroughgoing and effective regulation, which shall be based on a full knowledge of all the facts, including a physical valuation of property. This physical valuation is not needed, or, at least, is very rarely needed, for fixing rates; but it is needed as the basis of honest capitalization.

We have come to recognize that franchises should never be granted except for a limited time, and never without proper provision for compensation to the public. It is my personal belief that the same kind and degree of control and supervision which should be exercised over public service corporations should be extended also to combinations which control necessaries of life, such as meat, oil, and coal, or which deal in them on an important scale. I have no doubt that the ordinary man who has control of them is much like ourselves. I have no doubt he would like to do well, but I want to have enough supervision to help him realize that desire to do well.

I believe that the officers, and, especially, the directors, of corporations should be held personally responsible when any corporation breaks the law.

Combinations in industry are the result of an imperative economic law which cannot be repealed by political legislation. The effort at prohibiting all combination has substantially failed. The way out lies, not in attempting to prevent such combinations, but in completely controlling them in the interest of the public welfare. For that purpose the Federal Bureau of Corporations is an agency of first importance. Its powers, and, therefore, its efficiency, as well as that of the Interstate Commerce Commission, should be largely increased. We have a right to expect from the Bureau of Corporations and from the Interstate Commerce Commission a very high grade of public service. We should be as sure of the proper conduct of the interstate railways and the proper management of interstate business as we are now sure of the conduct and management of the national banks, and we should have as effective supervision in one case as in the other. The Hepburn Act, and the amendment to the Act in the shape in which it finally passed Congress at the last session, represent a long step in advance, and we must go yet further.

There is a widespread belief among our people that, under the methods of making tariffs which have hitherto obtained, the special interests are too influential. Probably this is true of both the big special interests and the little special interests. These methods have put a premium on selfishness, and, naturally, the selfish big interests have gotten more than their smaller, though equally selfish, brothers. The duty of Congress is to provide a method by which the interest of the whole people shall be all that receives consideration. To this end there must be an expert tariff commission, wholly removed from the possibility of political pressure or of improper business influence. Such a commission can find the real difference between cost of production, which is mainly the difference of labor cost here and abroad. As fast as its recommendations are made, I believe in revising one schedule at a time. A general revision of the tariff almost inevitably leads to log-rolling and the subordination of the general public interest to local and special interests.

The absence of effective state, and, especially, national, restraint upon unfair money getting has tended to create a small class of enormously wealthy and economically powerful men, whose chief object is to hold and increase their power. The prime need is to change the conditions which enable these men to accumulate power which it is not for the general welfare that they should hold or exercise. We grudge no man a fortune which represents his own power and sagacity, when exercised with entire regard to the welfare of his fellows. Again, comrades over there, take the lesson from your own experience. Not only did you not grudge, but you gloried in the promotion of the great generals who gained their promotion by leading the army to victory. So it is with us. We grudge no man a fortune in civil life if it is honorably obtained and well used. It is not even enough that it should have been gained without doing damage to the community. We should permit it to be gained only so long as the gaining represents benefit to the community. This, I know, implies a policy of a far more active governmental interference with social and economic conditions in this country than we have yet had, but I think we have got to face the fact that such an increase in governmental control is now necessary.

No man should receive a dollar unless that dollar has been fairly earned. Every dollar received should represent a dollar's worth of service rendered—not gambling in stocks, but service rendered. The really big fortune, the swollen fortune, by the mere fact of its size acquires qualities which differentiate it in kind as well as in degree from what is possessed by men of relatively small means. Therefore, I believe in a graduated income tax on big fortunes, and in another tax which is far more easily collected and far more effective—a graduated inheritance tax on big fortunes, properly safeguarded against evasion and increasing rapidly in amount with the size of the estate.

The people of the United States suffer from periodical financial panics to a degree substantially unknown among the other nations which approach us in financial strength. There is no reason why we should suffer what they escape. It is of profound importance that our financial system should be promptly investigated, and so thoroughly and effectively revised as to make it certain that hereafter our currency will no longer fail at critical times to meet our needs.

It is hardly necessary for me to repeat that I believe in an efficient army and a navy large enough to secure for us abroad that respect which is the surest guarantee of peace. A word of special warning to my fellow citizens who are as progressive as I hope I am. I want them to keep up their interest in our internal affairs; and I want them also continually to remember Uncle Sam's interests abroad. Justice and fair dealing among nations rest upon principles identical with those which control justice and fair dealing among the individuals of which nations are composed, with the vital exception that each nation must do its own part in international police work. If you get into trouble here, you can call for the police; but if Uncle Sam gets into trouble, he has got to be his own policeman, and I want to see him strong enough to encourage the peaceful aspirations of other peoples in connection with us. I believe in national friendships and heartiest good will to all nations; but national friendships, like those between men, must be founded on respect as well as on liking, on forbearance as well as upon trust. I should be heartily ashamed of any American who did not try to make the American government act as justly toward the other nations in international relations as he himself would act toward any individual in private relations. I should be heartily ashamed to see us wrong a weaker power, and I should hang my head forever if we tamely suffered wrong from a stronger power.

Of conservation I shall speak more at length elsewhere. Conservation means development as much as it does protection. I recognize the right and duty of this generation to develop and use the natural resources of our land; but I do not recognize the right to waste them, or to rob, by wasteful use, the generations that come after us. I ask nothing of the nation except that it so behave as each farmer here behaves with reference to his own children. That farmer is a poor creature who skins the land and leaves it worthless to his children. The farmer is a good farmer who, having enabled the land to support himself and to provide for the education of his children, leaves it to them a little better than he found it himself. I believe the same thing of a nation.

Moreover, I believe that the natural resources must be used for the benefit of all our people, and not monopolized for the benefit of the few, and here again is another case in which I am accused of taking a revolutionary attitude. People forget now that one hundred years ago there were public men of good character who advocated the nation selling its public lands in great quantities, so that the nation could get the most money out of it, and giving it to the men who could cultivate it for their own uses. We took the proper democratic ground that the land should be granted in small sections to the men who were actually to till it and live on it. Now, with the water power, with the forests, with the mines, we are brought face to face with the fact that there are many people who will go with us in conserving the resources only if they are to be allowed to exploit them for their benefit. That is one of the fundamental reasons why the special interests should be driven out of politics. Of all the questions which can come before this nation, short of the actual preservation of its existence in a great war, there is none which compares in importance with the great central task of leaving this land even a better land for our descendants than it is for us, and training them into a better race to inhabit the land and pass it on. Conservation is a great moral issue, for it involves the patriotic duty of insuring the safety and continuance of the nation. Let me add that the health and vitality of our people are at least as well worth conserving as their forests, waters, lands, and minerals, and in this great work the national government must bear a most important part.

I have spoken elsewhere[3] also of the great task which lies before the farmers of the country to get for themselves and their wives and children not only the benefits of better farming, but also those of better business methods and better conditions of life on the farm. The burden of this great task will fall, as it should, mainly upon the great organizations of the farmers themselves. I am glad it will, for I believe they are all well able to handle it. In particular, there are strong reasons why the Departments of Agriculture of the various states, the United States Department of Agriculture, and the agricultural colleges and experiment stations should extend their work to cover all phases of farm life, instead of limiting themselves, as they have far too often limited themselves in the past, solely to the question of the production of crops. And now a special word to the farmer. I want to see him make the farm as fine a farm as it can be made; and let him remember to see that the improvement goes on indoors as well as out; let him remember that the farmer's wife should have her share of thought and attention just as much as the farmer himself.

Nothing is more true than that excess of every kind is followed by reaction; a fact which should be pondered by reformer and reactionary alike. We are face to face with new conceptions of the relations of property to human welfare, chiefly because certain advocates of the rights of property as against the rights of men have been pushing their claims too far. The man who wrongly holds that every human right is secondary to his profit must now give way to the advocate of human welfare, who rightly maintains

[3] In a speech at Utica, New York.

that every man holds his property subject to the general right of the community to regulate its use to whatever degree the public welfare may require it.

But I think we may go still further. The right to regulate the use of wealth in the public interest is universally admitted. Let us admit also the right to regulate the terms and conditions of labor, which is the chief element of wealth, directly in the interest of the common good. The fundamental thing to do for every man is to give him a chance to reach a place in which he will make the greatest possible contribution to the public welfare. Understand what I say there. Give him a chance, not push him up if he will not be pushed. Help any man who stumbles; if he lies down, it is a poor job to try to carry him; but if he is a worthy man, try your best to see that he gets a chance to show the worth that is in him. No man can be a good citizen unless he has a wage more than sufficient to cover the bare cost of living, and hours of labor short enough so that after his day's work is done he will have time and energy to bear his share in the management of the community, to help in carrying the general load. We keep countless men from being good citizens by the conditions of life with which we surround them. We need comprehensive workmen's compensation acts, both state and national laws to regulate child labor and work for women, and, especially, we need in our common schools not merely education in book learning, but also practical training for daily life and work. We need to enforce better sanitary conditions for our workers and to extend the use of safety appliances for our workers in industry and commerce, both within and between the states. Also, friends, in the interest of the workingman himself we need to set our faces like flint against mob violence just as against corporate greed; against violence and injustice and lawlessness by wage workers just as much as against lawless cunning and greed and selfish arrogance of employers. If I could ask but one thing of my fellow countrymen, my request would be that, whenever they go in for reform, they remember the two sides, and that they always exact justice from one side as much as from the other. I have small use for the public servant who can always see and denounce the corruption of the capitalist, but who cannot persuade himself, especially before election, to say a word about lawless mob violence. And I have equally small use for a man, be he a judge on the bench, or editor of a great paper, or wealthy and influential private citizen, who can see clearly enough and denounce the lawlessness of mob violence, but whose eyes are closed so that he is blind when the question is one of corruption in business on a gigantic scale. Also remember what I said about excess in reformer and reactionary alike. If the reactionary man, who thinks of nothing but the rights of property, could have his way, he would bring about a revolution; and one of my chief fears in connection with progress comes because I do not want to see our people, for lack of proper leadership, compelled to follow men whose intentions are excellent, but whose eyes are a little too wild to make it really safe to trust them. Here in Kansas there is one paper which habitually denounces me as the tool of Wall Street, and at the same time frantically repudiates the statement that I am a Socialist on the ground that that is an unwarranted slander of the Socialists.[4]

National efficiency has many factors. It is a necessary result of the principle of conservation widely applied. In the end it will determine our failu.e or success as a nation. National efficiency has to do, not only with natural resources and with men, but it is equally concerned with institutions. The state must be made efficient for the work which concerns only the people of the state; and the nation for that which concerns all the people. There must remain no neutral ground to serve as a refuge for lawbreakers, and especially for lawbreakers of great wealth, who can hire the

---

[4] The *Appeal to Reason*, a widely circulated socialist paper edited by Julius Augustus Wayland, "The One Hoss Editor." It purveyed a peculiarly populistic brand of socialist doctrine.

vulpine legal cunning which will teach them how to avoid both jurisdictions. It is a misfortune when the national legislature fails to do its duty in providing a national remedy, so that the only national activity is the purely negative activity of the judiciary in forbidding the state to exercise power in the premises.

I do not ask for overcentralization; but I do ask that we work in a spirit of broad and far-reaching nationalism when we work for what concerns our people as a whole. We are all Americans. Our common interests are as broad as the continent. I speak to you here in Kansas exactly as I would speak in New York or Georgia, for the most vital problems are those which affect us all alike. The national government belongs to the whole American people, and where the whole American people are interested, that interest can be guarded effectively only by the national government. The betterment which we seek must be accomplished, I believe, mainly through the national government.

The American people are right in demanding that New Nationalism, without which we cannot hope to deal with new problems. The New Nationalism puts the national need before sectional or personal advantage. It is impatient of the utter confusion that results from local legislatures attempting to treat national issues as local issues. It is still more impatient of the impotence which springs from overdivision of governmental powers, the impotence which makes it possible for local selfishness or for legal cunning, hired by wealthy special interests, to bring national activities to a deadlock. This New Nationalism regards the executive power as the steward of the public welfare. It demands of the judiciary that it shall be interested primarily in human welfare rather than in property, just as it demands that the representative body shall represent all the people rather than any one class or section of the people.

I believe in shaping the ends of government to protect property as well as human welfare. Normally, and in the long run, the ends are the same; but whenever the alternative must be faced, I am for men and not for property, as you were in the Civil War. I am far from underestimating the importance of dividends; but I rank dividends below human character. Again, I do not have any sympathy with the reformer who says he does not care for dividends. Of course, economic welfare is necessary, for a man must pull his own weight and be able to support his family. I know well that the reformers must not bring upon the people economic ruin, or the reforms themselves will go down in the ruin. But we must be ready to face temporary disaster, whether or not brought on by those who will war against us to the knife. Those who oppose all reform will do well to remember that ruin in its worst form is inevitable if our national life brings us nothing better than swollen fortunes for the few and the triumph in both politics and business of a sordid and selfish materialism.

If our political institutions were perfect, they would absolutely prevent the political domination of money in any part of our affairs. We need to make our political representatives more quickly and sensitively responsive to the people whose servants they are. More direct action by the people in their own affairs under proper safeguards is vitally necessary. The direct primary is a step in this direction, if it is associated with a corrupt practices act effective to prevent the advantage of the man willing recklessly and un-scrupulously to spend money over his more honest competitor. It is particularly important that all moneys received or expended for campaign purposes should be publicly accounted for, not only after election, but before election as well. Political action must be made simpler, easier, and freer from confusion for every citizen. I believe that the prompt removal of unfaithful or incompetent public servants should be made easy and sure in whatever way experience shall show to be most expedient in any given class of cases.

One of the fundamental necessities in a representative govern-ment such as ours is to make certain that the men to whom the people delegate their power shall serve the people by whom they are elected, and not the special interests. I believe that every national officer, elected or appointed, should be forbidden to perform any service or receive any compensation, directly or indirectly, from interstate corporations; and a similar provision could not fail to be useful within the states.

The object of government is the welfare of the people. The material progress and prosperity of a nation are desirable chiefly so far as they lead to the moral and material welfare of all good citizens. Just in proportion as the average man and woman are honest, capable of sound judgment and high ideals, active in public affairs,—but, first of all, sound in their home life, and the father and mother of healthy children whom they bring up well, —just so far, and no farther, we may count our civilization a success. We must have—I believe we have already—a genuine and permanent moral awakening, without which no wisdom of legislation or administration really means anything; and, on the other hand, we must try to secure the social and economic legislation without which any improvement due to purely moral agitation is necessarily evanescent. Let me again illustrate by a reference to the Grand Army. You could not have won simply as a disorderly and disorganized mob. You needed generals; you needed careful administration of the most advanced type; and a good commissary —the cracker line. You well remember that success was necessary in many different lines in order to bring about general success. You had to have the administration at Washington good, just as you had to have the administration in the field; and you had to have the work of the generals good. You could not have triumphed without that administration and leadership; but it would all have been worthless if the average soldier had not had the right stuff in him. He had to have the right stuff in him, or you could not get it out of him. In the last analysis, therefore, vitally necessary though it was to have the right kind of organization and the right kind of generalship, it was even more vitally necessary that the average soldier should have the fighting edge, the right character.

So it is in our civil life. No matter how honest and decent we are in our private lives, if we do not have the right kind of law and the right kind of administration of the law, we cannot go forward as a nation. That is imperative; but it must be an addition to, and not a substitution for, the qualities that make us good citizens. In the last analysis, the most important elements in any man's career must be the sum of those qualities which, in the aggregate, we speak of as character. If he has not got it, then no law that the wit of man can devise, no administration of the law by the boldest and strongest executive, will avail to help him. We must have the right kind of character—character that makes a man, first of all, a good man in the home, a good father, a good husband— that makes a man a good neighbor. You must have that, and, then, in addition, you must have the kind of law and the kind of administration of the law which will give to those qualities in the private citizen the best possible chance for development. The prime problem of our nation is to get the right type of good citizenship, and, to get it, we must have progress, and our public men must be genuinely progressive.

The Nation and the States

Speech before the Colorado Legislature
29 AUGUST 1910

I was very much pleased by your invitation to me to address you to-day.[1] It is nearly twenty-nine years ago that I began my service in politics as a member of the Lower House of the New York State Legislature. I always felt that I graduated from Harvard, went into the New York Legislature, and began my education. I realize the great importance of the work of a state legislator, the difficulties under which he does that work, the temptations to which he is exposed; and I sympathize with the men who, having worked well, have the bitter knowledge that their good work has not been appreciated. If Colorado is at all like New York, there are occasional men who do not work well at all, and the extent of whose shortcomings should be practically appreciated more than it is. Since then, I have served in many different positions, including Governor and the position of Deputy Sheriff in the cow country under an employee of mine who was Sheriff; and, looking back, I can say with sincerity that I do not know any place where it is more necessary to have good work done, or where, together with bad work, there is more disinterested honest work done, than in the state legislatures of our country. Three or four

---

[1] The Republican Roosevelt had been invited to speak by the state legislature of Colorado, both houses of which were Democratic.

gentlemen to-day have expressed the hope that I would speak to you about some of your own troubles.[2] To relieve the obvious nervousness of the Assembly, I shall say that I am not going to do it, one reason being that, though each of those who addressed me felt very strongly that I should speak to you, each radically differed from all the others as to what I should say. There are troubles and failings connected with all legislative bodies about which I could speak; and of some of these I should speak to you now if I were not to make a speech this evening where I shall take them up at length.

I want now, as a man recently connected with the national government, to call attention to the great need that there shall be more coherent work in the future than in the past between the state and the national governments. The legislative and executive officers of our country, national and state, but, above all, the judicial officers, are to blame for the fact that there has grown up a neutral land—a borderland—in the spheres of action of the national and the state governments—a borderland over which each government tends to claim that it has the power, and as to which the action of the courts unfortunately has usually been such as to deny to both the power. Now, we have what I think is, on the whole, and with all its shortcomings and imperfections, the most satisfactory form of government that has yet been devised by men. I am accustomed to speak as a historian. There are plenty of defects in our system of government that I could point out; but, compared with the systems of government of other countries, good though some of them are, ours, I think, is the most satisfactory. One of the most valuable features is the largely realized effort to have the affairs that concern all of us throughout the land treated by the central or national legislature, while the affairs

[2] From October 1909 through May 1910, the muckraking magazine, *Everybody's,* had been running a sensational series of articles, "The Beast and the Jungle," by the nationally known Denver reformer, Judge Ben B. Lindsey. Lindsey charged that Colorado was controlled by a corrupt alliance of corporations and politicians.

which concern us only in each of our several localities are treated by our state legislatures. That is the wisest possible method so long as no areas are left uncovered by them; so long as there are no spaces that are not filled in by government control.

Unfortunately, the course of governmental construction by the courts, as also the course of governmental action by legislator and executive, has not kept pace in this nation during the last forty years with the extraordinarily complex industrial development. We have changed from what was predominantly an agricultural people, where all were on planes of livelihood not far apart, and where business was simple, into a complex industrial community with a great development of corporations, and with conditions such that by steam and electricity the business of the nation has become completely nationalized. In consequence, the needs have wholly changed. There was no need, in the old days, of the law taking special care of the rights of the farm laborer; for he could take care of himself, and, if he was not treated right, he could move on and take up a farm himself. If he did not succeed on a farm, he could go to a city, or he could go West. But at present the relations of employer and employee are wholly different from what they were before. We now have to protect the employee to a degree unnecessary half a century ago. We now have to recognize the desirability of the right of collective bargaining on the part of the employees face to face with the great corporation, as was not necessary when the employer was one man or a partnership of two or three men employing half a dozen or half a score of men. So a hundred years ago, when the sailboat and the canal boat and the wagon and the pack train represented the only means of communication, the states could each take care of the business within the state. Now, as we have had to recognize in laws for the control of railroad business and of other interstate business, the national government is obliged to act.

It happens, probably inevitably, that the courts occupy a position of importance in our government such as they occupy in no other government, because, instead of dealing only with the rights of one man face to face with his fellow men, as is the case with other governments, they here pass upon the fundamental governmental rights of the whole people as exercised through their legislative and executive officers. Unfortunately, the courts, instead of leading in the recognition of the new conditions, have lagged behind; and, as each case has presented itself, have tended by a series of negative decisions to create a sphere in which neither nation nor state has effective control; and where the great business interests that can call to their aid the ability of the greatest corporation lawyers escape all control whatsoever. Let me illustrate what I mean by a reference to two concrete cases. Remember that I believe in state's rights wherever state's rights mean the people's rights. On the other hand, I believe in national rights wherever national rights mean the people's rights; and, above all, I believe that in every part of our complicated social fabric there must be either national or state control, and that it is ruinous to permit governmental action, and especially judicial action, which prevents the exercise of such control. I am for a fact, not a formula; I am for the rights of the people first and foremost, and for the "rights" of the nation or state, in any given series of cases, just in proportion as insistence upon them helps in securing popular rights.

The first case to which I shall refer is the Knight Sugar Trust case.[3] In that case the Supreme Court of the United States handed down a decision which rendered it exceedingly difficult for the people to devise any method of controlling and regulating the business use of great capital in interstate commerce. It was a decision nominally against national rights, but really against popular rights—against the democratic principle of government by the people.

[3] *United States v. E. C. Knight Co.*, 156 U.S. 1 (1895). With only Justice Harlan dissenting, the Court ruled that the Sherman Act did not extend to combinations to control manufacture as distinguished from combinations to control commerce. This narrow interpretation of the statute dealt a heavy blow to the anti-trust movement.

The second case is the so-called New York Bakeshop case.[4] In New York City, as in most large cities, the baking business is likely to be carried on under unhygienic conditions—conditions which tell against the welfare of the general public. The New York Legislature passed, and the New York Governor signed, a bill remedying these unhealthy conditions. New York State was the only body which could deal with them; the nation had no power whatever in the matter. Acting on evidence which to them seemed ample and sufficient, acting in the interest of the public and in accordance with the demand of the public, the only governmental authority having affirmative power in the matter, the Governor and the Legislature of the State of New York, took the action which they deemed necessary, after what inquiry and study was needed to satisfy them as to the conditions and as to the remedy. The Governor and the Legislature alone had the affirmative power to remedy the abuse. But the Supreme Court of the United States possessed—and, unfortunately, exercised—the negative power of not permitting the abuse to be remedied. By a five to four vote they declared the action of the State of New York unconstitutional, because, forsooth, men must not be deprived of their "liberty" to work under unhealthy conditions.

All who are acquainted with the effort to remedy industrial abuses know the type of mind (it may be perfectly honest but is absolutely fossilized) which declines to allow us to work for the betterment of conditions among the wage earners on the ground that we must not interfere with the "liberty" of a girl to work under conditions which jeopardize life and limb, or the "liberty" of

[4] *Lochner v. New York*, 198 U.S. 45 (1905). In a 5-4 decision, the Supreme Court declared invalid a New York law which limited employment in bakeries to sixty hours a week and ten hours a day. The Court held that the statute denied the liberty of contract protected by the Fourteenth Amendment. In his famous dissenting opinion, Mr. Justice Holmes protested that the Court was reading its own economic theories into the Constitution. "The Fourteenth Amendment," he stated bluntly, "does not enact Mr. Herbert Spencer's *Social Statics*."

a man to work under conditions which ruin his health after a limited number of years.

Such was the decision. The court was, of course, absolutely powerless to make the remotest attempt to provide a remedy for the wrong which undoubtedly existed, and its refusal to permit action by the state did not confer any power upon the nation to act. The decision was nominally against state's rights, really against popular rights.

Such decisions, arbitrarily and irresponsibly limiting the power of the people, are of course fundamentally hostile to every species of real popular government. Representatives of the People of Colorado, here assembled in your legislative capacity, we as a nation should see to it that the people, through their several legislatures, national and state, have complete power of control in all matters that affect the public interest. There should be no means by which any man or set of men could escape the exercise of that control.

We should get the power; that is the first requisite. Now, then, the second is to see that the power be exercised with justice and moderation. The worst enemy of wise conservatism that I know is the type of conservative who tries to prevent wrongs from being remedied because the wrongs have existed for a long time; and, on the other hand, the worst enemy of true progress is the demagogue, or the visionary, who, in the name of progress, leads the people to make blunders such that in the resulting reaction they tend to distrust all progress. Distrust the demagogue and the mere visionary just as you distrust that hidebound conservative who too often, though an honest man himself, proves to be one of the most efficient friends of corruption. Remember that if you fall into the Scylla of demagogism, on the one hand, it will not help you that you have avoided the Charybdis of corruption and conservatism on the other. If you are in one gulf, it is perfectly true that you are not in the other. But you are in one.

Be progressive. A great democracy has got to be progressive, or it will soon cease to be either great or a democracy; but remem-

ber, no matter what your enthusiasm, that if you make rapid progress in the wrong direction you will merely have to undo it before
you get to the right path again. As I have said before, each one of
our localities has its own special problems to work out; and as
to those special problems, an outsider is not competent to speak;
but there are certain things to which all of us in every state should
pay heed, we in New York and you in Colorado, the people of
every state and the people of the national capital.

It I were asked to name the three influences which I thought were
most dangerous to the perpetuity of American institutions, I should
name corruption in business and politics alike, lawless violence, and
mendacity, especially when used in connection with slander.

Corruption: You cannot afford to tolerate in your ranks the corrupt man, and the first duty of a constituency should be to see that
its representative is not merely honest in the sense that he cannot
be legally shown to be dishonest, but that he is a dead straight man
whom no one can think of as crooked. I do not want it to be
praise to a man that he is honest; I want it to be an impossible
supposition for a representative to be thought of as anything else;
but you cannot get that honesty unless you insist upon it among
yourselves in your own relations of life. If you train up your children
to hear a shady scoundrel spoken of with a certain half admiration
as, "Well, he is smart"; if you let your children hear a man's
crookedness excused on the ground that he is clever, that he is a
cheat, but that he cheats mighty well, you have yourselves to blame
if your legislatures betray you. More than that, distrust anything in
the nature of class privilege; distrust the labor leader who will inveigh against corruption only when it is shown by the rich man;
and distrust equally the rich man who will subscribe heavily to put
down lawbreaking among small politicians, and who is shocked at
corruption among labor leaders, but who leaves you instantly as
soon as you try to bring the big corporation to book. If you elect a
man because you think he will be honest towards your class,—capi-

46

talists, farmers, laborers,—and if you are indifferent as to whether he is honest towards other people, you can make up your minds absolutely that he will betray you if he gets the chance. You cannot afford not to have a man honest all the way through, because if he is not, you do not know quite where the breaking down will come.

Lawless violence: Here again remember that in time of mob violence all reform has to wait until order is restored. As a people it is gravely to our discredit that there should be so much unpunished murder, so many deeds of lawlessness and mob violence. Let the friend of the people who is severe upon the corruption of wealth make up his mind that he is a mighty poor public servant if he does not set his face against disorder when it takes the form of violence, just as much as against corruption. The man who can only see evil in the corruption of the rich, and the man who can only see evil in the lawless violence of the poor, stand on the same plane of bad citizenship. Keep order. War both against corruption and against lawless violence. That is what you and public officials need to keep in mind.

Now as to critics. I don't like the thief, but I like the liar just as little. The very fact that we need to have corruption in every phase unflinchingly exposed, the very fact that we need to have every man shown up who has acted improperly, because it is not merely a disgrace but a vital injury to us to permit corruption in public life or corruption in business life, that very fact emphasizes the wrong done by the man who without warrant accuses another of corruption. He has committed one of the cardinal sins against the body politic. It is not merely an injury to the man accused, it is an injury of the deepest type to the body politic, because after awhile, when accusations are continually and sweepingly made against all men, good and bad, the public as a whole grow to believe in each accusation a little and in no accusation entirely, so that they grow to believe that there is a little something bad about the decent man and that there is not much bad about the crook. No greater harm can be done to the body politic than by those men who, through reckless and indiscriminate accusation of good men and bad men, honest men and dishonest men alike, finally so hopelessly puzzle the public that they do not believe that any man in public life is entirely straight; while, on the other hand, they lose all indignation against the man who really is crooked. Greatly though I scorn and despise the corrupt public servant, greatly though I wish to see him punished with the utmost severity of the law, my scorn and contempt for him are no greater than for the man who by mendacity and through slander attacks the character of honest men just as he attacks the character of dishonest men, and thereby does his best, be that best great or small, to tear down the pillar of the temple and bury us all under the ruins. I speak of the man who writes in the daily press. [*Loud applause.*] I trust that it is not because this is a legislative assembly that you have applauded this more than what I said about public officials! Now, I will go with you to the last point in condemning the man who in the public press writes an untruth, if you will go with me to the last point in condemning equally actively the legislator who acts corruptly. Now, I will resume my sentence where I left off. I speak of the man who writes in the public press. I speak of the man who writes in the magazines.[5] I speak of the politician on the stump. [*A pause—silence.*] Applaud! [*Loud applause.*] I knew I would get it when I pointed out the need of it! Judge men not by the class to which they belong, but by their conduct as individuals. The only man who I think is a little more useful than the wise and honest public official is the wise and honest man in the press, and the only man who I think is a little more noxious than the dishonest public official is the untruthful man in the public press. I will make myself perfectly clear. I ask you to stand by the official who is honest; I ask you to stand by the newspaper man and magazine writer who truthfully exposes corruption; and I ask you to stand against the

[5] These remarks were interpreted as a criticism of Judge Ben Lindsey, but Roosevelt may not have had Lindsey in mind. In fact, Roosevelt refused to go on with his speech in Denver Auditorium that same day until Lindsey, who had not received a ticket, had been sent for and invited to the platform.

official scoundrel who is dishonest and his equally base brother in the press who falsely accuses an honest man of dishonesty.

I thank you for the patience with which you have listened to me, and I am very glad I finally got all the applause I wanted at the points I wanted it.

Conservation

Speech at Denver before the Colorado Live Stock Association
29 AUGUST 1910

I was profoundly touched by the invitation to address you to-day. I have been profoundly touched by the reception in the city this morning; and, most of all, by the greeting I now receive and by the way that greeting has been phrased by the Governor and the Mayor.[1] I value it all the more inasmuch as they and I do not belong to the same party; because there are many things that stand infinitely above party; because when we come to the great essentials —to the things that make in their aggregate the character of a good citizen—we come to the things which dwarf parties and classes into absolute insignificance.

And now, my friends, I came here expecting to make an address on Conservation to an audience of perhaps fifteen hundred people specifically interested in it; and I only hope that you will have patience with me because I cannot travel as far afield as I would like in addressing an audience like this.

And, first, let me make clear what I do not mean by Con-

---

[1] The speech to the Colorado Live Stock Association was Roosevelt's third major address in Denver that day. Roosevelt had "a bully time" in Denver. All day long the streets of the city were thronged with cheering crowds. Both Democratic Mayor Robert W. Speer and Democratic Governor John F. Shafroth had praised Roosevelt warmly. When Speer suggested that the country might once more turn to the Colonel in 1912, the crowd waved flags and handkerchiefs and roared its approval.

servation. Conservation, as I use the term, does not mean nonuse or nondevelopment. It does not mean tying up the natural resources of the states. It means the utilization of these resources under such regulation and control as will prevent waste, extravagance, and monopoly; but at the same time, not merely promoting, but encouraging such use and development as will serve the interests of the people generally.

And if any man can point out where by the action of those who think as I do the development of the natural resources is being held up, I will join with him against my friends and followers and do my best to see that the development is not interfered with; but I want him to be sure of the facts before he comes. I wish you would read the report of Mr. Graves, of your Chamber of Commerce here, when charges affecting the Forestry Department and its alleged withholding of agricultural lands were made—and they were very grave and very large charges until it was required that they should be made definite, and then they dwarfed until they became well-nigh invisible. I will go with you to the limit in trying to alter any legislation or administration that improperly prevents the development of the natural resources; but when you come and tell me about it, tell me about the act itself—give me specific facts and not general accusations.

It is time we should wake up the country as to the need of using foresight and common sense as regards our natural resources. We of this generation hold the land in part for the use of the next generation, and not exclusively for our own selfish enjoyment. Mr. Mayor, in building up Denver, you had been thinking of it with an eye, not merely to your own administration, not merely to the welfare of the citizens now living, but with an eye to the welfare of the Denver that is to be. Governor, you are serving, not only for the Colorado now, but for the Colorado of your children's children —of those who are not voters to-day. So it must be with us as a whole in dealing with the natural resources. We have passed the time when we will tolerate the man whose only idea is to skin the country and move on. As it is with him, so it is with the nation. That farmer is a good citizen who leaves his farm improved, and not impaired, for his children; and he is a bad citizen if he has used up his farm and passes it on to his children who inherit it. So, the nation behaves well if it treats the natural resources as assets which it must turn over to the next generation increased, and not impaired, in value; and behaves badly if it leaves the land poorer to those who come after it. That is all I mean by the phrase, Conservation of natural resources. Use them; but use them so that as far as possible our children will be richer, and not poorer, because we have lived.

In the second place, these natural resources must be developed promptly, completely, and in orderly fashion. I am no friend of holding off. Development is an indispensable part of the Conservation plan. The forests, the mines, the water powers, and the land itself must be put in use. Those err who think that the opposite course is advocated by any whom I regard as genuine friends of Conservation.

In the third place, and so far as possible, these resources must be kept for the whole people and not handed over for exploitation to any single individual or group of individuals. We do not intend to discourage individual enterprise by diminishing unwisely the reward for that enterprise. On the contrary, we believe that the men of exceptional abilities should have exceptional rewards up to, but not beyond, the point where the reward becomes disproportionate to the services, up to the point where the abilities are used to the detriment of the people as a whole. I honor the captain of industry, and I am glad to see him rewarded so long as he acts honestly and so long as his reward is not wholly disproportionate to the work he has done. If he does not act honestly, then I hope the laws will be so framed and so administered as to go at him just as if he were the smallest sneak thief in the slums of a great city. And if his reward is utterly disproportionate to his great services, then I will join with those who try to shape conditions so that the reward and the services shall stand in better relation. What I say of the individual applies to the corporation. I am for the corporation which does right. I recognize the absolute need of the corporation in our business life to-day. I believe the corporation is entitled to protection in its rights; but it is not entitled to vote, and it is not entitled to proprietorship in any public man. We are for the liberty of the individual up to, and not beyond, the point where it becomes inconsistent with the welfare of the community. Thus, our consistent aim is to favor the actual settler—the man who takes as much of the public domain as he himself can cultivate, and there makes a permanent home for his children who come after him; but we are against the man, no matter what his ability, who tries to monopolize, at the expense of such settler, large masses of public land.

State and Federal Control

Now, to preserve the general welfare, to see to it that the rights of the public are protected, and the liberty of the individual secured and encouraged consistent with this welfare, and curbed when it becomes inconsistent therewith, it is necessary to invoke the aid of the government. There are points in which this governmental aid can best be rendered by the states; that is, where the exercise of state's rights helps to secure popular rights; and where this is true— where state's rights mean popular rights—I believe in state's rights. But there are large classes of cases where only the authority of the national government will secure the rights of the people; and where this is the case, I am a convinced and throughgoing believer in the rights of the national government. Let me take an example in connection with Conservation. Big business is no longer an affair of any one state. Big business has become nationalized, and the only effective way of controlling and directing it and preventing the abuses in connection with it is by having the people nationalize the governmental control in order to meet the nationalization of the big business itself. People speak as if it were an innovation to nationalize control by the government of big business. The innovation came on the part of the business men who nationalized their businesses. All we wish to do on behalf of the people is to meet the nationalization of the big business by nationalized government control. All commerce on a scale sufficiently large to warrant any control over it by the government nowadays is interstate or foreign commerce; and until this fact is heartily acknowledged and acted upon by both courts and legislative bodies, national and state alike, the interest of the people will suffer.

In the matter of Conservation, I heartily approve of state action where, under our form of government, the state, and the state only, has the power to act. I cordially join with those who desire to see the state, within its own sphere, take the most advanced position in regard to the whole matter of Conservation. I have taken exactly this attitude in my own state of New York. Unfortunately, in the East we are more backward than the West. Where the state alone had the power to act, I have done all I could to get it to act in the most advanced manner; and where the nation could act, I have done all I could to get national action in the same direction. Unfortunately, in the East, in this matter we have paid the penalty of not having our forest lands under national control; and the penalty has been severe. At this moment, states in New England, states in the Southeast, and the states through which the Appalachian Mountains run are paying the penalty of the inability of their state governments to do what they know ought to be done. The forests in the White Mountains and in the Appalachian ranges are being maltreated because they are under the control of eastern state governments; and we are doing our best by legislation in Congress at this moment, through the help of the western senators and congressmen, to get back the national control over those forests which the nation ought to have;[2] and as the penalty of undertaking this control so late, the nation will be put to an expense of millions of dollars to

[2] On March 1, 1911, Congress passed the Weeks Act which authorized the Federal Government to acquire land in the East for national forests.

get from the control of states that which the whole nation ought always to hold under the control of the national government. Most of the states—although they are old states—have not protected their forests, each failing to act by itself, because the action was really the common concern of all; and where action is the common concern of all, experience has shown that it can only be profitably undertaken by the national government.

As a result of the impossibility of getting such wise action by the several state governments in the East, we are doing our best to get national legislation under which the national government, at the expense of millions of dollars, shall undertake to do as regards the Appalachians and White Mountains of the East what it is now doing in the Rocky Mountains here out West. It would be both a calamity and an absurdity for the national government now to fail to do in the West the very thing that at a heavy pecuniary cost it is trying to do in the East. By actual experience in the East we have found to our cost that the nation, and not the several states, can best guard the interests of the people in the matter of the forests and the waters; and I am at this moment doing all I can to increase in the East the power of the national government at the expense of the power of the several state governments of the eastern states, because we have found by bitter experience that only thus can we adequately protect our natural resources. If the national government fails to attempt this duty at the outset, it will later on have to pay heavily in order to be allowed to take up the work, which, because it is done so late, cannot be so well done as if it had been begun earlier.

Water Power

Take the question of the control of the water power sites. The enormous importance of water power sites to the future industrial development of this country has only been realized within a very few years. Unfortunately, the realization has come too late as regards some of the power sites; but many yet remain with which our hands are free to deal. We should make it our duty to see that hereafter the power sites are kept under the control of the general government for the use of the people as a whole. Now, my fellow citizens, I wish I could impress upon you the importance of acting in that matter now. You still have the power. If you do not act now, your children will rage fruitlessly because they have lost the power to act with effect, and will be driven to propose radical and revolutionary measures if the time for taking moderate measures has been allowed to go by. True conservatism is that conservatism which is also the embodiment of the wise spirit of progress. It is that conservatism which acts conservatively before that has happened which will inflame men to madness. The fee should remain with the people as a whole, while the use is leased on terms which shall secure an ample reward to the lessees; which shall encourage the development and use of the water power, but which shall not create a permanent monopoly or permit the development to be antisocial, to be in any respect hostile to the public good. Keep the fee so that our children shall be able to determine for themselves what they will do about the water powers in the end.

There is something fairly comic in the appeal made by many of these men in favor of state control when you realize that the great corporations seeking the privileges of developing the water power in any given state are at least as apt to be owned outside that state as within it. In this country nowadays capital has a national and not a state use. I remember when it became our duty when I was President to move against the Northern Securities Company, against railroads running through Wisconsin, Montana, Idaho, and Oregon.[3] We found that the corporation was a corporation of what

[3] After a costly battle for control of western railroads between one financial empire headed by J. P. Morgan and James J. Hill and another headed by Edward H. Harriman and Jacob H. Schiff, the two rival empires agreed to a cease-fire which called for the creation of the Northern Securities Company in which both interests would be represented. In one of the first bold moves of his presidential administration, Roosevelt, in 1902, ordered his Attorney General to institute proceedings to dissolve this super-trust.

state? Of New Jersey! They had been paying heed to state's rights, and so it was left to New Jersey to protect the rights of Wisconsin and Montana. The great corporations which are managed and largely owned in the old states are those which are most in evidence in developing and using the mines and water powers and forests of the new territories and the new states, from Alaska to Arizona. Now, don't misunderstand me. These great corporations can do good. I am heartily with them in their proposal to develop these mines, and I wish to see the men at the head of them receive ample reward for the work they do. All that I ask—I do not ask it, I demand it—on behalf of the people is that these corporations submit to such supervision and control as shall insure that, together with the development, together with the benefit to the men making the development, there shall go good to the public to whom belong the resources that have been developed.

I have been genuinely amused during the past two months at having arguments presented to me on behalf of certain rich men from New York, and even Ohio, for instance, as to why Colorado and other Rocky Mountain states should manage their own water power sites.[4] Now, many of these men may be good citizens according to their lights; but naturally enough their special interest obscures their sense of the public need; and as their object is to escape an efficient control, exercised in the interest of all the people of the country, they clamor to be put under the state instead of under the nation. If we are foolish enough to grant their requests, we shall have ourselves to blame when we wake up to find that we have permitted another privilege to entrench itself and another portion of what should be kept for the public good to be turned over to individuals for purposes of private enrichment. During the last session of Congress, bills were introduced to transfer the water power sites

[4] Several weeks later, Roosevelt claimed that these remarks, directed at the actions of the Central Colorado Power Company, "put an instant stop to the proceeding." In fact, Senator Reed Smoot introduced a bill on behalf of the corporation in the very next session of Congress.

in the national forests and the public domain to the control of the states. I cannot state too strongly my belief that these measures are unwise and that it would be disastrous to enact them into law. In substance, their effect would be to free these great special interests from all effective control. The passage of such a bill would be a victory of the special interests over the general welfare, and a long backward step down the hill of progress we have of late been climbing.

Our people have for many years proceeded upon the assumption that the nation should control the public land. It is to this assumption of national outlook that we owe our wisest land legislation, from the Homestead Law to the Irrigation Law. The wise use of our public domain has always been conditioned upon national action. The states can greatly help, but the nation must take the lead, as regards the land, as regards the forests and waters; and perhaps peculiarly in the case of the waters, because almost all streams are really interstate streams.

Coal Lands

The same principle applies with peculiar force to the coal lands, and especially to the coal lands in Alaska, whose protection and ownership by the Federal Government is so necessary, both for full and free industrial development in the West and for the needs of our fleet in the Pacific. The coal mines should be leased, not sold, and those who mine the coal should pay back a part of the profits to the people. Now, understand me again. I would have them leased in such quantities and on such terms as will guarantee an ample reward to the lessee; and I would see such control kept in the hands of the general government as shall insure the work to the lessee accruing not only to his advantage, but to the advantage of the people of the states. It is the right and duty of the people to demand the most vigilant trusteeship on the part of that branch of the Federal Government in charge of the fuel resources of the United States.

The Neutral Ground

Remember also that many of the men who protest loudly against effective national action would be the first to turn round and protest against state action, if such action in its turn became effective, and would then unhesitatingly invoke the law to show that the state had no constitutional power to act. I have had experience with this attitude. As Governor of New York I fought for the passage of the franchise tax, and the men from the city railroads came to me and said, "If you turn us over to the localities, each locality will tax us to the death; each county or city will try to get out of us improperly as much money as they can, and we will be ruined. If we must be put under government control, let it be under the control of the state." I concluded that they were right; and got the bill passed. Almost before the ink was dry, those same men turned round and started legal procedure to declare that the act was unconstitutional because they had been put under state and not local control! Long experience has shown that it is by no means impossible, in cases of constitutional doubt, to get one set of judicial decisions which render it difficult for the nation to act, and another set which render it impossible for the state to act. In each case the privileged beneficiaries of the decision invoke the aid of those who treat the Constitution, not as a healthy aid to growth, but as a fetish to prevent growth; and they assail the advocates of wise and cautious progress as being opponents of the Constitution. Those of you who are old enough will remember that in 1860 and 1861 Abraham Lincoln was denounced as having violated the Constitution because, as his opponents stated, while it was undoubtedly unconstitutional to secede, it was equally unconstitutional to interfere with secession. As I have said before, I am a strong believer in efficient national action, where such action offers the best hope of securing and protecting the interest of the whole people as against the interest of a few. But I am emphatically in favor of state action where state action will best serve the purpose; and I am no less emphatically in favor of cordial and hearty coöperation between the nation and the state where their duties are identical or overlap.

If there is one thing which is more unwise than another, it is the creation by legislation, by executive, or by judicial action of a neutral ground in which neither the state nor the nation has power, and which can serve as a place of refuge for the lawless man, and especially for the lawless man of great wealth, who can hire the best legal talent to advise him how to keep his abiding place equally distant from the uncertain frontiers of both state and national power.

The Open Range

I am here at the invitation of the Colorado Live Stock Association; and I desire to express my appreciation of their steadfast stand for decency and progress in the handling of public lands and national forests. They have met and overcome the unrelenting opposition of some of the most influential stockmen of the state; they have won because they have been right. I want to express also my appreciation of the work of the American National Live Stock Association. It has been one of the really important forces working toward effective railroad legislation, while its support of the policy of Federal range control has given it a large place in national affairs. As an old time stockman, I realize that the present order of things on the open range cannot continue, and that the sure way to protect the range itself, prevent the increase of big outfits, promote the equitable use of the grazing lands, and foster genuine homestead settlement, is to extend over the open range a system of range control somewhat similar to that now in effect in the national forests.

Whatever system of range control may be adopted in detail, there are two things it must not do. It must not handicap or exclude the small man by requiring him to spend more money for fences than he can afford, and it must leave every acre that can be settled by bona fide homesteaders freely open to such settlement. If you find it excludes any small man, and you will bring any specific facts to me, I will do my best to remedy it. In speaking to this audience I do not suppose that there is a very large proportion of the homestead men present; but I know that all of you agree with me that it is the homestead men, the small settlers, the actual homemaker, whose interests we must do most to preserve. I do not believe that a single acre of our public lands should hereafter pass into private ownership, except for the single purpose of homestead settlement; and I know that the stockmen stand with me in their desire to remove every obstacle from the path of the genuine homesteader, and to put every possible obstacle in the pathway of the man who tries to get public lands by misrepresentation or fraud. This is absolutely necessary on the agricultural lands. It is at least equally necessary on the mineral lands. It would be a calamity whose baleful effect on the average citizen we can scarcely exaggerate, if the great stores of coal and other mineral fuels still owned by our people in Alaska and elsewhere should pass into unregulated ownership of monopolistic corporations.

The Forest Service

You progressive stockmen have stood heartily by the Conservation movement, and with you have stood many others throughout the West, to whom large credit is due, such as the lumbermen in Washington and Oregon, the irrigators in California, and the supporters of the country life movement in and around Spokane. I want to make my acknowledgments in particular to the Colorado Forestry Association, which has supported the forest work of the government with such unselfish zeal. The Forest Service has enemies because it is efficient. It would have no enemies if it did not do anything. Some of its best work has been met by the bitterest opposition. For example, it has done a real service by blocking the road against the grabbers of water power for themselves, and again by standing like a rock against the demands of bogus mining concerns to exploit the national forests. I have always done my best to help the genuine miner. I believe that one of the first duties of the government is to encourage honest mining on the public lands. But it is equally important to enforce the law firmly against the particularly dangerous class which makes its living off the public through fraudulent mining schemes.

I have already spoken of the claims made without justification that the Forest Service keeps the actual homesteader out of the enjoyment of the agricultural lands. Much of the opposition to the Forest Service, like much of the opposition to Conservation, takes the form of direct misrepresentation. For example, the cry is often heard that the national forests inclose great areas of agricultural land, which are thus put beyond the reach of settlement. This statement seems plausible only till the facts are known. In the first place, Congress has especially provided that whatever agricultural lands there may be in any national forest shall be open, under proper safeguards, to homestead settlement. And in the second place, when the opponents of Conservation are asked to point out the great stretches of inclosed agricultural land on the ground and in the presence of experts, instead of in speeches in a hall, they fail.

The Reclamation Service

The National Irrigation Congress is to hold a session in the city of Pueblo late in September. I am keenly sorry that I could not have accepted the invitation to be present; but you in Denver will pardon me if I put you first. I could have gone to Pueblo; but in order to make my engagements possible to fulfill them it was out of the question for me to go back to Colorado at this time. I sincerely regret it. I have never been to Colorado but that I have enjoyed myself. I must, however, be in the East at that time. But since I cannot be present then to express my keen, long-held, and deep-felt interest in the reclamation of arid lands by the Federal Government, I desire to do so now. There is no more effective instrument for the making of homes than the United States Reclamation Service, and no government bureau while I was President had reached a higher standard of efficiency, integrity, and devotion to the public welfare.

Like the Forest Service, the Reclamation Service has clashed with certain private interests, and has had to pay the penalty of its service to the public in the form of bitter opposition from those with whose profit it has interfered. The cry has been raised against it that the government must not do for its citizens at a less cost what private interests are ready to make them pay for at higher prices. And those of you who have been connected with getting a water supply for a big city know what kind of opposition that is to be encountered. Now, I believe fully in the private development of irrigation projects which the government cannot undertake. There is a large and legitimate field for such work. But the essential thing is to make homes on the land rather than to enable individuals to profit from the necessities of the men who make those homes. Now, I put the issue straight. If you believe primarily in the mere amassing of money in the aggregate by the citizens of the state, then you are right in supporting a system under which money will be made by private corporations which distribute the water at the expense of the users. If you believe, as far as may be just, in the welfare of the average citizen, you will favor a system that will give him, as long as he works hard and deserves it, the first chance of getting water from the government at as near cost price as may be. There is no more warrant for objection to the reclamation of arid lands by the government than there would be for protest against the government for patenting agricultural lands directly to the actual settler instead of settling them in block through a middleman who could make a profit from the transaction. The men who assert their right to get something for themselves at the cost of the community instead of by service to the community we have always had with us, and doubtless we always shall have; but there is no reason why we should yield to them. The Reclamation Service has not done so, and that is the chief reason for the attacks upon it.

I do not think that there is one among you who is a better and a more thoroughgoing Westerner than I am. There has been no support given to the Conservation policies so welcome as that which came from the West, and none in the West more welcome than that which came from Colorado. There are men and organizations in Colorado, and I mention Delta in particular, whose support of the Conservation policies has been of the greatest value to the nation. It has not always been an easy thing for them to stand for what was right; to stand for the real ultimate good as against the seeming temporary good; but they have stood for it steadily, nevertheless.

I have told you how we are working in the East trying to make good our mistakes; that now we have bills for passage through the national legislature endeavoring to get back for the nation the control which other bills have been introduced to do away with in the West. Gentlemen for whom I have personally the friendliest feelings introduced bills to try to get the nation to do in the West the very things which we are now proposing that the nation shall pay many millions of dollars to undo in the East.

From the standpoint of Conservation the East has wasted much of its own superb endowment; and as an American, as a lover of the West, I hope that the West will profit by the East's bitter lesson, and will not repeat the mistakes of the East. The East has wasted its resources; it suffers from the effect of this waste, which now puts it at a disadvantage compared to the West, and it is sorry. Most of the capital and very many of the men now attempting to monopolize your western resources are from the East. The West should learn the lesson of the East's mistakes; and it should remember that Conservation in the West will help the West first and most, and that the movement for Conservation is most earnest, most vigorous, and most effective in the West and among western men. That is one strong reason why the Conservation policy has come to stay.

I have just come back from a very interesting trip in the Old World. I spent a year of comparative holiday in Africa, and a quarter of a year of fairly vigorous work in Europe, during most of which it seemed to be the kind purpose of my hosts to make me feel thoroughly at home. [*Laughter and applause.*]

Although I have always felt a genuine friendliness for foreign peoples, and have come back with that feeling increased, yet I feel thankful that I can with sincerity say that with all our faults and shortcomings—and I know them well, and have striven to help in correcting a certain number of them in my time—there is not anywhere else on the face of the earth a land where life is so supremely well worth living, where the chance for the average man is as good, as it is here. [*Cheers.*] There is any amount that needs to be improved—and I do not think much of you if you simply cheer the fact that I say you are mighty good people, and then go home and do not try to make things better; but I think it is perfectly possible to combine a full knowledge of the evil that exists, not only with a determination to cut out that evil, but with a clear understanding of the great good that exists also. There were two things that struck me especially abroad. One was that, to the average man with whom life had gone hard, America stood as a name that symbolized hope; that symbolized the golden chance of allowing a man or woman to lead his or her life fully and freely to the utmost possible advantage to himself or herself and to his or her fellow men and women. America stood as a name of hope to the average man on the other side.

But there is this also that was true. Almost every man whom I met on the other side and conversed with, and who was a well-wisher of America, would after a while ask me anxiously about some features of national corruption in America, of business corruption or of political corruption; and every reactionary, every enemy of democratic government, every opponent of free institutions hailed with sardonic laughter each and every such instance of corruption in business or in politics as proof that it was an empty dream to believe that people can govern themselves honestly, wisely, and well. It is probably true that if we are unwilling to insist on honesty for our own sakes, we shall not do it for the sake of others; and yet, my friends, I think that we here should realize that we are not only custodians of the hopes of our children, but that in a peculiar sense we are custodians of the hope of the world; and shame, triple shame, is ours if we shatter the ideal of the world by shattering the world's belief in the possibilities of popular government on a continental scale. And I ask that you here do not confine yourselves simply to hearing me and enjoying a little thrill of pleasure over the sentiments expressed, but that you, men and women of Colorado, will go back to your homes and your daily lives with the resolute purpose to war for honesty in its deepest and broadest significance both in our business and in our politics; not only for our own sake, not only for the sake of our children who inherit the land after us, but for the sake of the peoples of the world who stand and watch this great experiment of free democracy in the West, so that their hope shall not be dead.

Natural Resources

Speech at St. Paul

6 SEPTEMBER 1910

Minnesota has almost always taken the lead in any great work, and Minnesota has been one of the first to take hold of the Conservation policy in practical shape; and she has done a great work and set an admirable example to the rest of us.[1] It is a work well set forth in your Governor's address yesterday;[2] and I am glad this Congress is held in such a state where we can listen to such an address made by a Governor who has a right to make it. Much that I have to say on the general policy of Conservation will be but a repetition of what was so admirably said on this general policy by the President of the United States yesterday.[3] In particu-

[1] Roosevelt spoke before a tempestuous convention of the National Conservation Congress badly divided between ardent advocates of conservation who favored a strong role for the federal government and a minority states' rights faction which supported a more cautious course. In this "red-hot conservation speech," Roosevelt aligned himself with the nationalist faction at the Congress. The delegates, delighted by Roosevelt's strong stand, interrupted almost every sentence he spoke with cheers.

[2] Governor Eberhard of Minnesota had stressed the importance of improved farm methods. Even a small increase in productivity of the soil, he had pointed out, would yield a great increase in national wealth.

[3] In fact, Roosevelt was unhappy about some of Taft's remarks. Although the President had supported conservation in his speech to the Congress, he had dissociated himself from the "rhapsodies" of the conservationists. Taft's statement, "In these days there is a disposition to look too much to the Federal Government for everything," was regarded as an indirect statement of support of the states' rights faction and a fling at Roosevelt's New Nationalism.

lar all true friends of Conservation should be in heartiest agreement with the policy which the President laid down in connection with the coal, iron, and phosphate lands; and I am glad to see that at its last session Congress finally completed the work of separating the surface title to the land from the mineral beneath it.

Now, my friends, America's reputation for efficiency stands deservedly high throughout the world. We are efficient probably to the full limits that are permitted any nation to attain by the methods hitherto used. The average American is an efficient man who can do his business; and it is recognized throughout the world that this is so. There is great reason to be proud of our achievements; and yet no reason to believe that we cannot excel our past. Through a practically unrestrained individualism, we have reached a pitch of literally unexampled material prosperity, although the distribution of this prosperity leaves much to be desired from the standpoint of justice and fair dealing. But we have not only allowed the individual a free hand, which was in the main right; we have also allowed great corporations to act as though they were individuals, and to exercise the rights of individuals, in addition to using the vast combined power of high organization and enormous wealth for their own advantages. This development of corporate action, it is true, is doubtless in large part responsible for the gigantic development of our natural resources, but it is not less responsible for waste, destruction, and monopoly on an equally gigantic scale.

The method of reckless and uncontrolled private use and waste has done for us all the good it ever can; and it is time to put an end to it before it does all the evil it easily may. We have passed the time when heedless waste and destruction and arrogant monopoly are longer permissible. Henceforth we must seek national efficiency by a new and better way, by the way of the orderly development and use, coupled with the preservation, of our natural resources, by making the most of what we have for the benefit of all of us, instead of leaving the sources of material prosperity open to indiscriminate exploitation. These are some of the reasons why it is wise that we should abandon the old point of view, and why Conservation has become a great moral issue in becoming a patriotic duty.

Waterways

One of the greatest of our Conservation problems is the wise and prompt development and use of the waterways of this nation. There are classes of bulky freight which can always go cheaper and better by water if there is an adequate waterway; and the existence of such a type of waterway in itself helps to regulate railroad rates. The Twin Cities, lying as they do at the headwaters of the Mississippi, are not upon the direct line of the proposed Lakes-to-the-Gulf deep waterway. And yet Minnesota, with its vast iron resources and its need of abundance of coal, has peculiar interest in that problem; and the Twin Cities, therefore, have their own personal concern in the deepening and regulation of the Mississippi to the mouth of the Missouri and to the Gulf. I have spoken of how progressive Minnesota is and how progressive these cities are; but there are other progressive cities in the West, too. I have just come from Kansas City. The merchants there have themselves undertaken, by raising more than a million dollars, to start the improvement of the waterway at their door, so that they shall be able to benefit by it. It is sometimes said that the waterway projects are backed by people who are delighted to see the government spend its money, but who are not willing to show their faith in the proposition by spending their own. Kansas City is spending its own. The project for a great trunk waterway, an arm of the sea, extending from the Gulf of Mexico to the Great Lakes, should not be abandoned. A report theron in full should be made to the government, so that the government can act in the interest of the whole people and without regard to the pressure of special interests. But, subject to the action of such a body, the Lakes-to-the-Gulf deep waterway, and the development of the rivers which flow into it, should be pushed to completion vigorously and without delay.

But we must recognize at the outset that there are certain conditions without which the people cannot hope to derive from it the benefits they have a right to expect. In nearly every river city from St. Paul to the Gulf the water front is controlled by the railways. Nearly every artificial waterway in the United States, either directly or indirectly, is under the same control. It goes without saying that (unless the people prevent it in advance) the railways will always attempt to take control of our waterways as fast as they are improved and completed. I do not mention this to blame them in the least, but to blame us for permitting them to do so. If Uncle Sam cannot take care of himself, then there is no particular reason why any railroad man should act as his guardian, and if he attempted the feat, he would merely find himself alone among other railroad men, and Uncle Sam would not be materially benefited. Uncle Sam has got to do the job himself. We must see to it that adequate terminals are provided in every city and town on every improved waterway, terminals open under reasonable conditions to the use of every citizen and rigidly protected against monopoly; and we must compel the railroads to coöperate with the waterways continuously, effectively, and under reasonable conditions. Unless we do so, the railway lines will refuse to deliver freight to the boat lines, either openly or by imposing prohibitory conditions; and the waterways, once improved, will do comparatively little for the benefit of the people who pay the bill.

Adequate terminals properly controlled and open through lines by rail and boat are two absolutely essential conditions to the usefulness of inland waterway development. I believe, furthermore, that the railways should be prohibited from owning, controlling, or carrying any interest in the boat lines on our rivers, unless under the strictest regulation and control of the Interstate Commerce

Commission, so that the shipper's interests may be fully protected.[4]

Now, here another word in supplement. You, the people, ought not to sit supine and let the railroads gain control of the boat lines and then turn around and say that the men at the head of the railroads are very bad people. If you leave it open to them to control boat lines, some of them are sure to do so; and it is to our interest that the best among them should do so. Don't let any of them do it, excepting under conditions we lay down. In other words, when you of your own fault permit the rules of the game to be such that you are absolutely certain to get the worst of it at the hands of some one else, don't blame the other man; change the rules of the game.

Drainage

Take the question of drainage. It is almost as important in certain states as irrigation is in other states. Where the drainage area of the swamp and overflow lands is wholly within the lines of a particular state it may be well, at least for the present, to leave the handling of it to state or private action; but where such a drainage area is included in two or more states, the only wise course is to have the Federal Government act.[5] Land should be deeded from the state back to the Federal Government, and it then should take whatever action is necessary. Much of this work must be done by the nation in any case as an integral part of inland waterway development. It affords a most promising field for cooperation between the states and the nation.

[4] The railroad king, James J. Hill, sat on the platform. As Roosevelt began to emphasize the need for federal control of the railroads, he turned directly to Hill to make his point.

[5] Roosevelt interpolated these remarks about drainage into his prepared speech. On the previous day, Taft had said that federal action would be unconstitutional. Roosevelt's statement on drainage drew the lines sharply between the two men.

The National Forests

The people of the United States believe in the complete and rounded development of inland waterways for all the useful purposes they can be made to serve. They believe also, as you here in Minnesota have done, in forest protection and forest extension. The fight for our National Forest in the West has been won, and if, after winning it, we now go ahead and lose it, that is our affair. We are not going to do it. After a campaign in which the women of Minnesota did work which should secure to them the perpetual gratitude of their state, Minnesota won her National Forest, and will keep it; but the fight to create the Southern Appalachian and White Mountain Forests in the East is not yet over. The bill has passed the House, and will come before the Senate for a vote next February. The people of the United States, regardless of party or section, should stand solidly behind it, and see that their representatives do likewise. And, friends, in the East, thanks to the fact that our ancestors did not have sufficient foresight, the nation is now being obliged to spend great sums of money to take back from the eastern states what those eastern states have shown themselves unable adequately to protect and handle. I have been a Governor of an eastern state myself, and we of the states of the East could not do the work as well as the national government, and we are now permitting the national government to take these lands and do the work. In the light of what we are now doing in the East it seems to me the wildest folly to ask us to start in the West to repeat the same blunders that are now being remedied. My language shall at least be free from ambiguity.

If any proof were needed that forest protection is a national duty, the recent destruction of forests in the West by fire would supply it. Even with the aid of the army added to that of the Forest Service, the loss has been severe. Without either it would have been vastly greater.

But the Forest Service does more than protect the national forests against fire. It makes them practically and increasingly useful as well. During the last year for which I have the figures, the national forests were used by 22,000 cattlemen, with their herds, 5000 sheepmen, with their flocks, 5000 timbermen, with the crews, and 45,000 miners; and yet people will tell you that they have been shut up from popular use. More than 5000 persons used them for other special industries. Nearly 34,000 settlers had the free use of wood. The total resident population of the national forests is about a quarter of a million, which is larger than the population of certain states. More than 700,000 acres of agricultural land have been patented or listed for patent within the forests, and the reports of the forest officers show that more than 400,000 people a year use the forests for recreation, camping, hunting, fishing, and similar purposes. All this is done, of course, without injury to the timber, which has a value of at least a thousand million dollars. Moreover, the national forests protect the water supply of a thousand cities and towns, about 800 irrigation projects, and more than 300 power projects, not counting the use of water for these and other purposes by individual settlers. I think that hereafter we may safely disregard any statements that the national forests are withdrawn from settlement and use.

A Country Life Institute

The investigations of the Country Life Commissions[6] have led the farmers of this country to realize that they have not been getting their fair share of progress and all that it brings. Some of our farming communities in the Mississippi Valley and in the middle West have made marvelous progress, yet even the best of them, like communities of every other kind, are not beyond improvement,

[6] In 1908 Roosevelt named a Country Life Commission to investigate rural life and make recommendations on rural problems. The work of the Commission quickened interest in the national rural life movement led by men like Liberty Hyde Bailey.

while much needs to be done in some other sections to improve country life. As yet we know comparatively little of the basic facts of rural civilization, compared with those of industrial life. The means for better farming we have studied with care; but to better living on the farm and to better business on the farm the farmers themselves have given scant attention. I mean by that, having the farmer use the middleman where it is to the farmer's advantage to do so, and not to be used by the middleman chiefly to the advantage of the middleman. One of the most urgent needs of our civilization is that the farmers themselves should undertake to get for themselves a better knowledge along these lines, and then to apply it. Sir Horace Plunkett, an Irishman, for many years a Wyoming cattleman and now devoting himself in Ireland to the country life problem there, has suggested in his recent book on the "Country Life Problem in America" the creation of a Country Life Institute as a center where the work and knowledge of the whole world concerning country life may be brought together for the use of every nation.[7] I am strongly in sympathy with this idea, and hope to see it carried out with the coöperation and assistance of our own people. Last spring, while visiting the capital of Hungary—Buda-Pesth—I was immensely impressed by the Museum of Country Life, containing an extraordinary series of studies in agriculture, in stock-raising, in forestry, in mining. It was one of the most interesting places I have ever visited. The exhibits were of the utmost practical importance, and were also intensely interesting and instructive. I felt rather ashamed that I, a citizen of what we suppose to be a "very go-ahead country," should be in Hungary obliged to confess we had nothing at all like that in our own country. I greatly wish we had such a museum in Washington; and some of your farmer congressmen ought to get a full and detailed report of this Buda-Pesth museum to be printed for distribution in a public document.

[7] Sir Horace Plunkett (1854-1932), a leader of the farm co-operative movement in Ireland, was a frequent visitor to America. His study, *The Rural Life Problem of the United States*, was published in 1910.

I would like to see a study made of such museums, so that we may take what is good of them for our own use in America.

Human Efficiency

As a people we have not yet learned to economize. One of the virtues we Americans need is thrift. It is a mere truism to say that luxury and extravagance are not good for a nation. So far as they affect character, the loss they cause may be beyond computation. But in the material sense there is a loss greater than is caused by both extravagance and luxury put together. I mean the needless, useless, and excessive loss to our people from premature death and avoidable diseases. Wholly apart from the grief, suffering, and wretchedness which they cause, the material loss each year has been calculated at nearly twice what it costs to run the Federal Government. In addition to the state and city health officers and organizations, there is urgently needed a Federal Bureau of Health, to act, so far as the national government properly may, to relieve our people from this dreadful burden.

The National Conservation Commission

One of the most important meetings in our recent history was that of the Governors in the White House in May, 1908, to consider the Conservation question. By the advice of the Governors the meeting was followed by the appointment of a National Conservation Commission. The meeting of the Governors directed the attention of the country to Conservation as nothing else could have done, while the work of the Commission gave the movement definiteness and supplied it with a practical program. Now, my friends, so far I have had nothing but praise to speak of Minnesota. I cannot continue to speak only words of praise. At the moment when the Commission was ready to begin the campaign for putting its program into effect, an amendment to the Sundry Civil Bill was introduced by a congressman from Minnesota with the purpose to put a stop to the work so admirably begun.[8] Congress passed the amendment. Its object was to put an end to the work of a number of commissions, which had been appointed by the President, and whose contribution to the public welfare had been simply incalculable. Among these were the commission for reorganizing the business methods of the government, the Public Lands Commission, the Country Life Commission, and the National Conservation Commission itself. When I signed the Sundry Civil Bill containing this amendment, I transmitted with it as my last official act a memorandum declaring that the amendment was void, because it was unconstitutional interference with the rights of the Executive, and that if I were to remain President, I would pay to it no attention whatever.

The National Conservation Commission thereupon became dormant. The suspension of its work came at a most unfortunate time, and there was serious danger that the progress already made would be lost. At this critical moment the National Conservation Association was organized. It took up the work which otherwise would not have been done. If it had not done it, we would not have had this meeting here; and it exercised a most useful influence in preventing bad legislation, in securing the introduction of better Conservation measures at the past session of Congress, and in promoting the passage of wise laws. It deserves the confidence and support of every citizen interested in the wise development and preservation

[8] In his years in the White House, Roosevelt had established a number of conservation agencies without Congressional sanction and had found ingenious ways to finance their work. In February, 1909, he had asked Congress for funds for the work of the National Conservation Commission. Congress had not only refused the request but had adopted the Tawney amendment to the Sundry Civil Bill which forbade any federal administrator to aid any executive commission not authorized by Congress. On the day before Roosevelt's speech in St. Paul, Gifford Pinchot, the apostle of the conservation movement, had spoken in support of the opponent of Representative James A. Tawney of Minnesota, Chairman of the House Committee on Appropriations and sponsor of the amendment.

of our natural resources, and in preventing them from passing into the hands of uncontrolled monopolies. It joins with the National Conservation Congress in holding this meeting. I am here by the joint invitation of both.

Pan-American Conservation

When the government of the United States awoke to the idea of Conservation and saw that it was good, it lost no time in communicating the advantages of the new point of view to its immediate neighbors among the nations. A North American Conservation Conference was held in Washington, and the coöperation of Canada and Mexico in the great problem of developing the resources of the continent for the benefit of its people was asked and promised. The nations upon our northern and southern boundaries wisely realized that their opportunity to conserve the natural resources was better than ours, because with them destruction and monopolization had not gone so far as they had with us. So it is with the republics of Central and South America. Obviously, they are on the verge of a period of great material progress. The development of their natural resources—their forests, their mines, their water, and their soils—will create enormous wealth. It is to the mutual interests of the United States and our sister American republics that this development should be wisely done. Our manufacturing industries offer a market for more and more of their natural wealth and raw material, while they will increasingly desire to meet the demand in commercial exchange. The more we buy from them, the more we shall sell to them. Their prosperity is inseparably involved with our own. Thank Heaven, we of this hemisphere are now beginning to realize, what in the end the whole world will realize, that normally it is a good thing for a nation to have its neighbor nations prosper. We of the United States are genuinely and heartily pleased to see growth and prosperity in Canada, in Mexico, in South America.

I wish I could impress upon certain small republics of the South, whose history has not always been happy, that all we desire is that they shall be prosperous and peaceful. We do not want to interfere; it is particularly a thing we dislike to do. All that we ask of any nation on this continent is that it shall be prosperous and peaceful, able to do reasonable justice within its own boundaries to the stranger within its gates; and any nation able to do that can count upon our heartiest and most cordial support.

It is clear that unless the governments of our southern neighbors take steps in the near future by wise legislation to control the development and use of their natural resources, they will probably fall into the hands of concessionaires and promoters, whose single purpose, without regard to the permanent welfare of the land in which they work, will be to make the most possible money in the shortest possible time. There will be shameful waste, destructive loss, and shortsighted disregard of the future, as we have learned by bitter experience here at home.

Unless the governments of all the American republics, including our own, enact in time such laws as will both protect their natural wealth and promote their legitimate and reasonable development, future generations will owe their misfortunes to us of to-day. A great patriotic duty calls upon us. We owe it to ourselves and to them to give the American republics all the help we can. The cases in which we have failed should be no less instructive than the cases in which we have succeeded. With prompt action and good will the task of saving the resources for the people is full of hope for us all.

State and Federal Control

But while we of the United States are anxious, as I believe we are able, to be of assistance to others, there are problems of our own which must not be overlooked. One of the most important

Conservation questions of the moment relates to the control of the water power monopoly in the public interest. There is apparent to the judicious observer a distinct tendency on the part of our opponents to cloud the issue by raising the question of state as against Federal jurisdiction. We are ready to meet this issue, if it is forced upon us. But there is no hope for the plain people in such conflicts of jurisdictions. The essential question is not one of hairsplitting legal technicalities. It is not really a question of state against nation. It is really a question of special corporate interests against the popular interests of this nation. If it were not for those special corporate interests, you never would have heard of the question of state as against the nation. The question is simply this: Who can best regulate the special interests for the public good? [9] Most of the great corporations, and almost all of those that can be legitimately called the great predatory corporations, have interstate affiliations. Therefore, they are out of reach of effective state control, and fall of necessity within the Federal jurisdiction. One of the prime objects of those among them that are grasping and greedy is to avoid any effective control, either by state or nation; and they advocate at this time state control simply because they believe it to be the least effective. If it should prove effective, many of those now advocating it would themselves turn round and say that such control was unconstitutional. I had my own experience. I will give you an example of it. When I was Governor of New York there came up a bill to tax the franchises of certain big street railway corporations. As originally introduced, the bill provided that the taxation should be imposed by the several counties and localities in which those corporations did business. Representatives of the corporations came to me and said that this was going to work a great hardship upon them; that the state authority would be more just than the local authority; especially if a railroad were to run

[9] "You can do it yourself," someone in the gallery cried out. The crowd howled in delight.

through two or three towns or counties, they would each endeavor to get the whole benefit of the whole taxation for their own locality; and, in the name of justice, I ought to agree to have the state, and not the localities, made the taxing power. I thought their plea just, and recommended and sanctioned the change, and the bill was made a law; and those same corporations instantly entered suit against it upon the ground that it was unconstitutional,—that it was unconstitutional to take the power of taxation away from the localities and give it to the state—and they carried the suit up to the Supreme Court, where, during my own term as President, it was decided against them. In the great fight of the people to drive the special interests from the domination of our government, the nation is stronger, and its jurisdiction is more effective, than that of any state.

And now I want to say another thing which the representatives of those corporations did not at the moment believe, but which, I am sure, in the end they will find out: because of the fact that the Federal Government is better able to exact justice from them, I also believe that it is less apt in some sudden gust of popular passion to do injustice to them.

I want you to understand my position. I do not think that you will misunderstand it. I will do my utmost to secure the rights of every corporation. If a corporation is improperly attacked, I will stand up for it to the best of my ability. I would stand up for it even though I were sure that the bulk of the people were misguided enough for the moment to take the wrong side and be against it. I should fight hard to see that the people, through the national government, did full justice to the corporations; but I do not want the national government to depend upon their good will to get justice for the people. Most of these great corporations are in a large part financed and owned in the Atlantic states, and it is rather a comic fact that many of the chief and most serious upholders of states' rights in the present controversy are big business men who live in other states. The most effective weapon is Federal laws and the Federal executive. That is why I so strongly oppose the demand to turn these matters over to the states. It is fundamentally a demand against the interest of the plain people, of the people of small means, against the interest of our children and our children's children; and it is primarily in the interest of the great corporations which desire to escape effective government control.

And I ask you to consider two more things in connection with this. Waters run. They do not stay in one state. That fact seems elementary; but it tends to be forgotten. I have just come from Kansas. Practically all the water in Kansas runs into Kansas through another state, and out of it into other states. You cannot have effective control of a watershed unless the same power controls all the watersheds. Sometimes the water actually runs out of one country into another. One of the great irrigation projects of Montana has been delayed because waters that make the Milk River rise in Montana, flow north into Canada, and then come back into Montana. You cannot settle the matter except through the national government. Take the experience of other nations. Take the experience of the little republic of Switzerland. It actually tried what some of our people wish to try; it actually tried the experiment of letting each canton handle its own water; and the conflict of jurisdiction wrought so much injustice that it became necessary about nine years ago for the national government to assume control of the waters of Switzerland on the explicit ground that all of the waters belonged to all of the citizens of the Swiss nation. Now, I am not asking that we go ahead recklessly; but I am only asking that we do not go backward where other countries have gone ahead.

The Conservation Fight

As the President yesterday pointed out, one of the difficulties that we have to meet in our fight for putting into practice the Conservation idea is that our aim is continuously misrepresented, that the effort is made to show that we are anxious to retard development. It has been no slight task to bring before ninety million people a great conception like that of Conservation, and convince them that it is right. This much we have accomplished; but there remains much to be cleared up, and many misunderstandings to be removed. These misunderstandings are due in part at least to direct misrepresentation by the men to whose interest it is that Conservation should not prosper. For example, we find it constantly said by men who should know better that temporary withdrawals, such as the withdrawals of coal lands, will permanently check development. Yet the fact is that these withdrawals have no purpose except to prevent the coal lands from passing into private ownership until Congress can pass laws to open them to development under conditions just alike to the public and to the man who will do the developing. Understand here, if there is any doubt as to whether the conditions are liberal enough to the men who are doing the developing, I would always solve the doubt in favor of liberality to those men. I want to give them every chance to do well for themselves, but I want to see that in doing well for themselves they also do well for the rest of us. If there is delay, the responsibility for it rests, not on the men who made the withdrawals to protect the public interests, but on those who prevent Congress from passing wise legislation and so putting an end to the need for withdrawals.

Abuses committed in the name of a just cause are familiar to all of us. Many unwise things are done and many unwise measures are advocated in the name of Conservation, either through ignorance, or by those whose interest lies not in promoting the movement, but in retarding it. For example, to stop water power development by needless refusal to issue permits for water power or private irrigation works on the public lands inevitably leads many men, friendly to Conservation and believers in its general principles, to assume that its practical application is necessarily a check upon progress. Nothing could be more mistaken. The idea, widely circulated of late, that Conservation means locking up the natural resources for the exclusive use of later generations, is wholly mistaken. Our purpose is to make full use of these resources, but to consider our sons and daughters as well as ourselves, just as a farmer uses his farm in ways to preserve its future usefulness. Conservation is the road to national efficiency, and it stands for wise and ample development.

But in spite of these difficulties, most of which are doubtless inevitable in any movement of this kind, Conservation has made marvelous progress. I have been astounded and delighted on my return from abroad at the progress made while I was away. We have a right to congratulate ourselves on this marvelous progress; but there is no reason for believing the fight is won. In the beginning, the special interests, who are our chief opponents in the Conservation fight, paid little heed to the movement, because they neither understood it nor saw that if it won they must lose. But with the progress of Conservation in the minds of the people, the fight is getting sharper. The nearer we approach to victory, the bitterer the opposition that we must meet and the greater the need for caution and watchfulness. Open opposition we can overcome, but I warn you especially against the men who come to congresses such as this, ostensibly as disinterested citizens, but actually as the paid agents of the special interests. I wish to say that I heartily approve of the attitude of any corporation which comes here openly and because it is interested in the deliberations of a meeting such as this; which comes hither to advocate, by its openly accredited agents, views which it believes the meeting should have in mind. I approve of the corporation that does that; and I would despise any of our people who feared instantly to give the most ample and respectful hearing and real consideration to any such plea thus put forward. The corporation, through its agents, not only has a right to be heard, but if it does not desire to be heard, we should see that its case should be presented. My protest is not against the man who comes here as the corporation againt, but against the man who comes here ostensibly for something else but really is for the corporation.

This congress is a direct appeal to the patriotism of our whole people. The nation wisely looks to such gatherings for counsel and leadership. Let that leadership be sound, definite, practical, and on the side of all the people. It would be no small misfortune if a meeting such as this should ever fall into the hands of the open enemies or false friends of the great movement which it represents.

Conclusion

It is our duty and our desire to make this land of ours a better home for the race; but our duty does not stop there. We must also work for a better nation to live in this better land. The development and conservation of our National Character and our free institutions must go hand in hand with the development and conservation of our natural resources, which the Governors' Conference so well called the foundation of our prosperity. Whatever progress we may make as a nation, whatever wealth we may accumulate, however far we may push mechanical development and production, we shall never reach a point where our welfare can depend in the last analysis on anything but the fundamental qualities of good citizenship—upon honesty, courage, and common sense. The homely virtues are the lasting virtues, and the road which leads to them is the road to genuine and lasting success.

What this country needs is what every free country must set before it as the great goal toward which it works—an equal opportunity for life, liberty, and the pursuit of happiness for every one of its citizens, rich and poor, great and humble alike. To achieve this end we must put a stop to the improper political dominion of the great special interests. This country, its natural resources, its natural advantages, its opportunities, and its institutions belong to all its citizens. They cannot be enjoyed fully and freely under any government in which the special interests as such have a voice. The supreme political task of our day, the indispensable condition of national efficiency and national welfare, is to drive the special interests out of our public life.

The Commission Principle

Speech at Sioux Falls
3 SEPTEMBER 1910

It is more than thirty years ago that I first came into what was then the territory of Dakota, and twenty-seven years ago that I ran my cattle on the Little Missouri.[1] The first occasion that I ever got into that part of the territory that is now the state of South Dakota was a couple of years later on, when about a dozen of us went down to the Indian roundup to hunt up cattle, and we came pretty near being run in by the Indian police. So that I came very close to making my first appearance in South Dakota under arrest.

My friends, I never can sufficiently express the obligations I am under to the territory of Dakota, for it was here that I lived a number of years in a ranch house in the cattle country, and I regard my experience during those years, when I lived and worked with my own fellow ranchmen on what was then the frontier, as the most important educational asset of all my life. It is a mighty good thing to know men, not from looking at them, but from having been one of them. When you have worked with them, when you have lived with them, you do not have to wonder how they feel, because you feel it yourself. Every now and then, I am amused when newspapers in the East,—perhaps, I may say, not always

---

[1] Roosevelt spoke in Sioux Falls, South Dakota to an immense throng tightly wedged together in a circus tent. The speech was notable because of the extensive attention he gave the tariff, a subject he skillfully avoided when president.

friendly to me,—having prophesied that I was dead wrong on a certain issue, and then finding out that I am right, express acid wonder how I am able to divine how people are thinking. Well, sometimes I don't and sometimes I do; but when I do it comes simply from the fact that this is the way I am thinking myself. I know how the man that works with his hands and the man on the ranch are thinking, because I have been there and I am thinking that way myself. It is not that I divine the way they are thinking, but because I think the same way.

Friends, I have come here to the West this time to visit the people I know so well and in whom I believe with all my heart, and to talk of certain things that interest none of us in a merely party sense, but do interest all of us as American citizens. Parties are good as instruments, and only as instruments. The thing that Americans should recollect is that what matters is not the opinions that divide them from one from another so much as it is the great fundamentals upon which they are united. We must have our differences; and it would be a very unhealthy thing if all of us thought alike. We need the friction with people different from ourselves; and my experience with my fellow countrymen is that there will always be plenty of them who will think different ways. We need the intellectual differences that come from such friction, and we must resolutely, but with mutual respect and forbearance among ourselves, battle for our respective opinions. That is good and wholesome; but it is not merely good and wholesome, but vital, to remember that on the really great issues we must all unite. Take what I mean when I speak of the "square deal." I mean not only that each man should act fairly and honestly under the rules of the game as it is now played, but I mean also that if the rules give improper advantage to some set of people, then let us change the rules of the game. Now, I make this discrimination between men. When a man cheats, if he swindles the public, if he corrupts a legislature, or if, as a member of the legislature, he tries to blackmail any one else, drive that man out of politics or business if you can; but when you find a man who is just like the rest of us, who tries to manage his business just about the same way as the rest of us manage ours; if you find that he has made a disproportionate fortune or has obtained other advantages which it is not healthy for the country that he should have, do not blame him—he has just done what the average citizen would have done in his place; do not blame him, but change the rules of the game.

Now, that has direct reference to the matter of the tariff. Whenever men just like ourselves—possibly not much better, but probably not in the least worse—continually fail to give us the results we have a right to expect from their efforts, we may just as well make up our minds that the fault lies, not in their personalities, but in the conditions under which they work; and profit comes, not from denouncing them, but from seeing that the conditions are changed. This is especially true of tariff making. It has been conclusively shown, by experiments repeated again and again, that the methods of tariff making by Congress, which have now obtained for so many years, cannot, from the very nature of the case, bring really satisfactory results. With the present tariff, made by the same methods as its predecessor and as that predecessor's predecessor, there is grave dissatisfaction.[2] The people know that there are some things in it which are not right, and therefore they tend to suspect the, as I think, more numerous things in it which are right. They know that the system on which it was made, the same system on which its predecessors were made, encourages a scramble of selfish interests, to which the all-important general interest of the public is necessarily more or less subordinated. There was a time when this scramble was regarded as the natural course in tariff making, and was not resented. The people demand, and rightly, that the profit of the special interests shall be subordinated to the general welfare in every case. It is this attitude—practically a new attitude—of the people which must be met in dealing with the present tariff, and

[2] Dissatisfaction with the Payne-Aldrich Tariff Act of 1909 had been the first in a series of incidents that had split the Republican Party.

with proposals to amend the present tariff. Very little improvement, indeed, will follow any attempt to revise the tariff by methods hitherto used. The thing to do is to change the methods. I believe that this country is fully committed to the principle of protection; but it is to protection as a principle; to protection primarily in the interest of the standard of living of the American workingman. I believe that when protection becomes, not a principle, but a privilege and a preference—or, rather, a jumble of privileges and preferences—then the American people disapprove of it. Now, to correct the trouble, it is necessary, in the first place, to get in mind clearly what we want; and, in the next place, to get in mind clearly the method by which we hope to obtain what we want. What we want is what I have already said—a square deal in the tariff as in everything else; a square deal for the wage earner; a square deal for the employer, and a square deal for the general public. To obtain it, we must have a thoroughly efficient and well-equipped tariff commission.

The tariff ought to be a material issue, and not a moral issue; but if, instead of a square deal, we get a crooked deal, then it becomes very emphatically a moral issue. What we desire—when I say "we" I am speaking of the American people—in a tariff is such a measure of protection as will equalize the cost of production here and abroad; and as the cost of production is primarily labor cost, this means primarily a tariff sufficient to make up for the difference in labor cost here and abroad. The American public wants the American laboring man put on an equality with other citizens, so that he shall have the ability to achieve the American standard of living and the capacity to enjoy; and to do this, we must see that his wages are not lowered by improper competition with inferior wage workers abroad—with wage workers who are paid poorly and who live as no Americans are willing to live. But the American public does not wish to see the tariff so arranged as to benefit primarily a few wealthy men.

As a means toward the attainment of the end in view, we have as yet devised nothing in any way so effective as a tariff commission. There should be a commission of well-paid experts; men who should not represent any special interest or industry; who should be masters of their subjects; men of the very highest character, who should approach the matter with absolute disregard of every outside consideration. I do not want to see these men of one party or another or of one trade or another; but experts, single-minded in finding out, and telling, the truth. These men should take up in succession each subject with which the tariff deals and investigate the conditions of production here and abroad; they should find out the facts and not merely accept the statements as to the facts of interested parties; and they should report to Congress on each subject as soon as the subject has been covered. Then, action can be taken at once on the particular schedule concerned, while the commission immediately proceeds to investigate another. By these means logrolling would be avoided, and each subject treated on its merits, while there would be no such shock to general industry as is implied in the present custom of making sweeping changes in the whole tariff at once. Finally, it should be the duty of some governmental department or bureau to investigate the conditions in the various protected industries, and see that the laborers really are getting the benefit of the tariff supposed to be enacted in their interest. And if, from an investigation of a certain industry, it appears that the tariff, supposed to be imposed for the benefit of the wage worker, results in such shape that the benefit does not reach him, the tariff on that industry should be taken off. Moreover, to secure good treatment abroad, we should keep the maximum and minimum provision.

I would apply the same principle of commission in another matter,—the improvement of the rivers and harbors. At present, a river and harbor bill, like a tariff bill, tends to be settled by a squabble among a lot of big selfish interests and little selfish interests, with scant regard to the one really vital interest, that of the country as a whole. In this matter the national legislature would do well to profit by the example of Massachusetts. Until within a year Massachusetts dealt with its land and harbor legislation just as in Washington the Federal tariff and river and harbor laws have been dealt with; and there was just the same pulling and hauling, the same bargaining and logrolling, the same subordination of the general interest to various special interests. Last year the Governor[3] took up the matter, and on his recommendation the legislature turned the whole business over to a commission of experts; and all trouble and scandal forthwith disappeared. Incidentally, this seems to me to be a first-class instance of progressive legislation.

And now, friends, the same principle that I believe should be applied in dealing with the tariff should be applied in the questions that come before us for settlement by legislation. I do not mean appointing a commission. I mean the principle of giving justice and demanding justice. Take corporations. A corporation that behaves well, that justifies itself by service to the public, should be well treated; and it is just as much our duty to hunt out of public life the corrupt public servant who seeks to blackmail a corporation as it is to hunt out the man who improperly and corruptly serves a corporation. Now, let me give you an example in my own experience here in the old territory of Dakota in the cattle days. In those days there were no fences in the cow country, and we kept track of our herds by branding each calf with the brand of the cow that it followed. I do not have to explain that to you; but I do to an Eastern audience; and there must be plenty of you who know what mavericks are. By range law at that time, when we found a maverick,—an unclaimed, unbranded yearling,—we would put on the brand of the ranch on which it was found. Close to me was a man with the Thistle brand. I had hired a new puncher, and was out with him one day on the range, and we struck a maverick. He got out his rope, we threw the maverick, I made a little of fire of sagebrush, and took a cinch ring and heated it to run on the brand. It was on the range, and I said to the puncher, "Put on the

[3] Governor Eben S. Draper of Massachusetts.

91

Thistle brand." He said, "All right, Boss; I know my business." "Hold on a minute," I said; "you are putting on my brand." He said, "I always put on the Boss's brand." And then I said, "Oh! all right; go back and get your time." He said, "What's that for?" And I said, "My friend, if you will steal for me, you will steal from me." And the same way with the public man. If he will steal for you, if he will act dishonestly on your behalf, he will steal from you and he will act dishonestly against you if he gets a chance. Do justice to the corporation. It is entitled to justice; but it is not entitled to own any man in public life. A this moment I think that the most important question of the various important questions before us is the divorce of big business from politics.

Each man of great wealth is entitled absolutely to the protection of the law. He is entitled to it exactly as much as the small man; and you are not to be excused if you do not give him as much as the small man; but neither are you to be excused if you give him more. Do you see what I mean? Remember that justice means justice to both sides. If there was danger of an assault on the property or person of any very rich man, even though he were only one of a not inconsiderable number of very rich men with whom I happen to get on badly—if there was danger of an assault on him in person or property, I would count myself a worthless American citizen if I did not come myself to his protection, and I would think the same of you. But after protecting him I would then do my level best, in company with the rest of my fellow citizens, to see that he did not have a chance to do anything crooked on his side. In other words, I believe that we should try to do entire justice to such a man and exact entire justice from him. Do not ever for one moment fix your eyes only on one particular kind of wrongdoing, or on one particular class of your fellow citizens as being wrongdoers. I know men, you know men, who will loudly inveigh against the corruption of the rich man; but you cannot get them—especially if they are politicians—just before election time to say anything against the violence of the mob for fear that they will hurt the feelings of the labor vote. I remember on one occasion being introduced as the poor man's friend. I said, "Now, let us amend that. I am the poor man's friend if the poor man is straight, and I am the rich man's friend if the rich man is straight; but if a man is crooked, I am against him, rich or poor." If a body of labor men commit a deed of violence,—turn themselves into a mob,—the first duty of decent citizens is to put down the violence and disperse the mob. You have got to have order and the supremacy of the law, or you cannot have civilization. If a rich man acts corruptly and dishonestly, if he arrogates privileges to himself, and disregards the rights of others, then it is our prime duty to punish that rich man and to make the conditions such that he cannot again repeat his offense.

Lawless violence and the corruption that eats into the vitals of honest government are equally dangerous to the welfare of the people. Under other forms of government there may be an appearance of success and an appearance of prosperity, even when the average citizen is not straight. It cannot be so with us. We here, we of this great democracy, we who are engaged in the greatest and most hopeful, and yet the most difficult, governmental experiment that has ever been tried—the experiment of securing self-government for a people on a continental scale—we cannot afford not to have the highest quality of individual citizenship. The stream will not rise higher than its source. If the average man is not a decent, straight man, knowing his rights and insisting upon them, and knowing his duties and performing them, we cannot have good government. Frown upon the corrupt man, frown upon the man who violates the law; and remember this, that if he steals in small things he will steal in big things if he gets the chance.

Send to represent you in public life men who are literally incorruptible, men who will not only not do what is wrong if tempted with money, but who will not do what is wrong even if tempted by popular applause. You have the right to have your representatives represent you; but, mind you, always remember that if you ask them to do what is wrong, you ask them to misrepresent all that is best in you.

Demand the highest ideals in your representatives, and shape your political action with two things in view.

In the first place, try to get by legislation, national and state, a better chance for the average man, a greater equality of opportunity for that man. This country is founded on the theory that it is a great deal better that the average man should have a good living than that the exceptional man should have a great profit. Shape your laws so that the man shall have a great profit only if he renders a great service to his fellows. We must have exceptional men, and we must give them exceptional rewards; but the rewards should bear some kind of proportion to the services rendered. I do not think that the American public grudges an exceptional reward to an exceptional man if it is commensurate with what he has done, but it does grudge it when he gets an exceptional reward for what is in its essence swindling, or when although he has rendered a service the reward is out of proportion to the service rendered.

It is a bad thing for our community if any considerable class of people lead their lives under conditions so hard that they cannot be good citizens. It is almost equally damaging to a man not to have enough work and to have so much that he is crushed under it. Our steady effort should be, so far as possible, to so shape the work of our lawmaking bodies as to help the average man and the average woman do their work under the most favorable conditions. Now that is the first thing we should do—do what we can by legislation and an honest administration of the laws to equalize conditions, to make opportunity really fairly equal for all men, and do away with conditions that tend to break down and depress any given set of workers. That is the first part.

Now, the second part is this: After everything has been done that can be done by legislation, remember that the fundamental factor in any man's success in life must be that man's own character. The wisest laws and the best government will not help a man who will not work, or who cannot work well and wisely. Every man of us stumbles at times; there is not one of us here who does not sometimes stumble, and who, therefore, ought not to have a helping hand stretched out to him. Shame upon us if we fail to stretch out a helping hand to the man who stumbles; but if he lies down, you cannot carry him. You can help him most by helping him to help himself.

Another thing. Let each man remember his rights, and also let him remember the rights of others; and especially let the man who is conscious of his wrongs see that he does not put any of them on the shoulders of the woman who happens to be his wife. I have met more than one agitator, whom you could always see in the crossroads store, inveighing against the inequality of the social system that kept him down, and all the while he lived at all only because his wife took in washing, or did something of that kind. Distrust also the man who would like to reform the whole world, but who cannot keep his family decently clothed and fed. The first duty of every man and woman is their duty in the family—to those nearest to them. If a man is not a good father, a good husband, he is a poor citizen. That is not enough; but he has got to be that or he is a poor citizen. Then, further. If he is not a good neighbor, if he is not a man you are willing to deal with, to work alongside of, he is not going to be of much good to the state at large.

If there is one day when it is our duty to serve the state, there are a hundred days when it is our duty to serve our families; but we ought all of us to be ready to serve the state when the day comes. Woe unto the nation which is unable to endure in such a season; woe unto the nation whose sons shrink from making a sacrifice that only heroic natures can make. Take an example from the men of the Civil War. I was proud to-day to have the National Guard here and see them march by. I have been a guardsman myself. I wished to see them because I like to see our men keep alive the spirit which enabled the men of the dark years of '61-'65 to do their duty.

And I want you to remember the lesson that they taught us. You may notice, friends, that I have not been promising you the millennium if you vote my way. I have not been telling you, and shall not tell you, that if you do your duty you will have a life of ease and pleasure. I do not think we shall have the millennium, but I think we are not to be excused if we do not try measurably to improve our condition. I am not advising you to act so as to make life more easy for you; I am not advising you to act in a spirit that shall disregard what is difficult; I am not advising you to get around obstacles; but I am advising you so that you can overcome them. I think all of you here know the unwise man,—I am sorry to say, as often the unwise woman,—who, because he or she has had a hard time in life, foolishly refuses to teach the children how best to meet the difficulties in life. It often happens that such a woman wishes her daughter "brought up like a lady," meaning thereby that the daughter shall be brought up a perfectly useless individual; and I think we all know rich men who leave to their sons riches which are millstones around their necks because they have brought them up to do nothing useful and to lead that most hopeless and dismal of all possible lives—a life devoted to pleasure as a business. It is not only the poorest business, but the funny thing is, they do not get any pleasure out of it.

Bring your children up not so that they will shirk difficulties, but so that they will overcome them; not so that they will try to have a soft time of selfish ease, but so that they will have the greatest joy that comes to mankind—the satisfaction of knowing, whenever the end may come, that they have led worthy lives.

Labor and Capital

Speech at Fargo

5 SEPTEMBER 1910

To-day[1]—on Labor Day—I speak in one sense to those especially personally and vitally interested in the labor struggle; and yet I speak of this primarily as one aspect of the larger social struggle growing out of the attempts to readjust social conditions and make them more equitable.

The nineteenth century was distinctly one of economic triumphs—triumphs in the domain of production, including transportation and the mechanics of exchange. The marvelous progress made during that hundred years in these respects multipled man's productive power to an almost inconceivable degree. In the matter of the production of wealth, as much progress was made during the nineteenth century as during all previous periods since history dawned. I am not speaking hyperbolically; I mean that literally. When this nation was founded, steam and electricity were unknown. Our whole modern industrial system had not yet come into being; and the means of transportation for men and goods were the same as those that were in existence in the time of Trajan's empire and the days of Egypt and Nineveh; that is, the changes brought on in a single century through machinery and steam have been greater

---

[1] Roosevelt spoke at the bottom of a natural amphitheater in Island Park; rain fell before he finished speaking.

than the sum total of the changes of the preceding thousands of years; and these very changes and this material progress have thrust upon us social and political problems of the first magnitude. The triumphs of the physical sciences in the nineteenth century represented progress primarily in the material elements of civilization. That was their problem; but the most pressing problems that confront the present century are not concerned with the material production of wealth, but with its distribution. The demands of progress now deal not so much with the material as with the moral and ethical factors of civilization. Our basic problem in the twentieth century is to see that the marvelously augmented powers of production bequeathed to us by the nineteenth century be made to administer to the needs of the many rather than be exploited for the profit of the few.

The American wage earner faces this larger social problem in a dual capacity: first, as a citizen of the republic charged with the full duty of citizenship; and, next, as a wage earner—as a wage worker—who, together with his fellow workers, is vitally concerned in the question of wages and general conditions of employment, which affect not only his well-being and that of his wife and children, but the opportunities of all workers for a higher development.

It is true of wage workers, as of all other citizens, that most of their progress must depend upon their own initiative and their own efforts. Nevertheless, there are three different factors in this progress. There is, first, the share which the man's own individual qualities must determine. This is the most important of all, for nothing can supply the place of individual capacity. Yet there are two other factors of prime importance, namely: what can be done by the wage workers in coöperation with one another, usually through unions; and what can be done by government—that is, by the instrument through which all the people work collectively. Wages and other most important conditions of employment must remain largely outside of government control; must be left for adjustment by free contract between employers and wage earners, subject—and I call your attention to the proviso—to legislation which will prevent conditions which compel men or women to accept wages representing less than will insure decent living. But to attempt to leave the question of contract between employer and employee merely to individual action means the absolute destruction of individualism; for where the individual is so weak that he, perforce, has to accept whatever a strongly organized body chooses to give him, his individual liberty becomes a mere sham and mockery. It is indispensably necessary, in order to preserve to the largest degree our system of individualism, that there should be effective and organized collective action. The wage earners must act jointly, through the process of collective bargaining, in great industrial enterprises. Only thus can they be put upon a plane of economic equality with their corporate employers. Only thus is freedom of contract made a real thing and not a mere legal fiction. There are occasional occupations where this is not necessary; but, speaking broadly, it is necessary throughout the great world of organized industry. I believe this practice of collective bargaining, effective only through such organizations as the trades unions, to have been one of the most potent forces in the past century in promoting the progress of the wage earners and in securing larger social progress for humanity. Wherever there is organized capital on a considerable scale I believe in the principle of organized labor and in the practice of collective bargaining, not merely as a desirable thing for the wage earners, but as something which has been demonstrated to be essential in the long run to their permanent progress. Where capital is organized, as it must be organized under modern industrial conditions, the only way to secure proper freedom—proper treatment—for the individual laborer is to have labor organize also.

This does not mean that I unequivocally indorse any or all practices that labor organizations may happen to adopt, or any or all principles that they may choose to enunciate. Labor organizations have the weaknesses and defects common to all forms of human organizations. When any man tells you that the laboring man never goes wrong, make up your minds that he is telling you what he knows to be an untruth, and distrust him accordingly; for it is a good old principle to act upon in the long run, that the most uncomfortable truth is a safer traveling companion than the pleasantest falsehood. Sometimes labor organizations act very well, and sometimes, like the rest of mankind, they act very badly; and I am for them when they act well, and I am against them when they act badly. I believe that their existence is a necessity; I believe that their aims and purposes are generally good; and I believe that all of them have occasionally made mistakes, and that some of them have been guilty of wrongdoing. Just in so far as they are strong and effective they tempt designing men who seek to control them for their own interests, and stimulate the desires of ambitious leaders who may be clever, crooked men, or who may be honest but visionary and foolish. In other words, in treating of labor unions, as in treating of corporations, or of humanity generally, we shall do well to remember Abraham Lincoln's saying that "there is a deal of human nature in mankind." Whether in a man or in an organized body of men, the power to do good means that such power may be twisted into evil; and in proportion as the power grows so it becomes steadily more important that it should be handled aright. Just in proportion as in its proper function power is important to social progress, so in its improper function it becomes fraught with social disaster.

Outside critics should appreciate the necessity of organized labor, and understand and sympathize with what is good in it instead of condemning it indiscriminately. On the other hand, those within its ranks should fearlessly analyze the criticisms directed against it, and ruthlessly eliminate from the practices of its organization those things which justify such criticism and attack. In other words, let the outsider realize the good—the necessity—of organized labor, and let the men within the organization realize the necessity of keeping the organization straight. This is the path, not only of right, but of wisdom and safety. Public opinion in the United States is daily becoming more alert and more intelligent and more forceful; and no organization, whether trades union or corporation, whether industrial or nonindustrial, can endure or permanently amount to a social force if it does not harmonize with a wise and enlightened public opinion. Hitherto we Americans have been over-occupied with material things, and have neglected to watch the play of the social forces about us. But now we are awakening from that indifference; and every form of organization representing an important economic, political, or social force must undergo a closer scrutiny than ever before.

I think that the next quarter of a century will be important politically in many ways (I do not use the word "Politically" in the way of party politics; but I am speaking of the social development of our people); and in none more so than in the labor movement. Not only are the benefits of labor organizations more clearly understood than before, but any shortcoming or vice displayed in connection therewith is also more clearly understood and more quickly resented. Just as it is with corporations, just so it is with railroads. Forty years ago the railroads could do with absolute impunity, and without any criticism, things which would cause well nigh a revolution if they attempted them now. The public is growing more and more to understand that, in a contest between employer and employee—a corporation and a trades union—not only the interests of the contestants, but the interests of the third party—the public— must be considered. Anything like levity in provoking a strike, on the one hand or on the other, is certain more and more to be resented by the public. Strikes are sometimes necessary and proper; sometimes they represent the only way in which, after all other methods have been exhausted, it is possible for the laboring man to stand up for his rights; but it must be clearly understood that a strike is a matter of last resort, and, of course, violence, lawlessness, and mob rule must be promptly and sternly dealt with, no matter what the cause may be that excites them. Our social organization is too complex for us to fail quickly to condemn those who, with levity or in a spirit of wanton brutality, bring about far-reaching and disastrous interference with normal processes. More and more we are growing to understand that corruption and lawless disorder are twin foes of the body politic, and that neither can be tolerated. All that I can do to help in bettering social conditions, to help in making things better for the man who has had a hard time in life, will be done; but when he resorts to lawless violence, when there comes a question of mob rule, all questions of reform must be left in abeyance until the laws are absolutely obeyed. The public sympathizes cordially with any movement for a good standard of living and for moderate hours of employment. (I personally, for instance, cordially believe in eight hours a day, and in one day in seven for complete rest.) Where men and women are worked under harsh and intolerable conditions, and can secure no relief without a strike, or, indeed, where the strike is clearly undertaken for things which are vitally necessary—and then only as a last resort in the effort to achieve the end in any other ways—public sympathy will favor the wage workers; but it will not favor them unless such conditions as these are fulfilled, and it will condemn them if they resort to lawless violence. Therefore, it is becoming more and more important that the labor movement should combine steady, far-seeing leadership with discipline and control in its ranks; and I am glad that this afternoon I can say, when I speak of the proper type of leadership, you have an instance in the gentleman who has spoken to us this afternoon on behalf of labor.[2] Dishonest leadership is a curse anywhere, but nowhere is it a greater curse than in the labor movement. If there is one lesson which I would rather teach my fellow Americans than any other, it is to hound down the dishonest man— no matter what his condition—and to brush aside with impatient contempt the creature who denounces dishonesty only when it is

[2] George B. Howley, president of the Minnesota and North Dakota Federation of Labor, who had declared: "There is not a man on the face of the earth who stands as near and dear to the labor people as Theodore Roosevelt."

found in some special social stratum. Hunt down the dishonest man without regard to class; and if he belongs to your class, hunt him down a little quicker. Take a case in politics. When I was President I sought so to carry myself that there should not be any need of saying, "Put the other party in to turn the rascals out," because I would turn them out myself. I will cinch the dishonest man of the other party; and if he is a member of my own party I will cinch him just a little bit quicker. Let the labor leader, the politician who needs the votes of the labor leaders, remember that it is their duty to hunt down the dishonest man in the labor movement; and let the man of means, the business man, the editor of the big paper that is financed by business men, remember that it is their duty to hunt down the dishonest man of great wealth.

I cannot help saying just a word more about the delight it gave me this afternoon to hear the utterances of a Federal judge who looks ahead,[3] a Federal judge who not only stands for honesty and righteousness in the conventional forms in which we have been accustomed to see them for generations, but who understands changed conditions and realizes that the Constitution of the United States must be administered, if it is to be administered wisely, by men who sympathize with, and understand, the needs of the wage worker, just as they sympathize with, and understand, the needs of all other American citizens.

For many years I have been more or less closely associated with representative leaders of labor, organized and unorganized. Some of these men are among my close friends, whom I respect and admire as heartily as I do any men in America. There are some of them to whom I go as freely for assistance and guidance, for aid and help, in making up my mind how to deal with our social problems, as I go to the leaders of any business or profession. I cannot pay too high a tribute to the worth and energy of these men—to their sincerity and good judgment as leaders. But no movement—no leader-

[3] C. F. Amidon, U.S. Judge for this district, had deplored the backwardness of the United States in the field of workmen's compensation legislation.

ship—however honest, can endure unless the rank and file live up to their duties, and search for such leadership and support it when they find it. If the best men in a labor union leave its management and control to men of a poorer type, the effect will be just as disastrous as when good citizens in a city follow the same course as regards city government. The stay-at-home man in a union is just as much responsible for the sins of omission and commission of his organization as the stay-at-home man in a city is for the civic conditions under which he suffers and about which he complains.

All that properly can be done should be done by all of us to help upward the standard of living and improve the ability of the average man to reach that standard. There are still in the United States great masses of skilled and unorganized labor whose conditions of work and living are harsh and pitiable. It is a shocking indictment of our industrial condition to be told in a matter-of-course way in a government report that thousands of workers in this country are compelled to toil every day in the week, without one day of rest, for a wage of $45 a month. Such a condition is bad for them, and, in the end, bad for all of us. Our commercial development should heartily be encouraged; but it must not be allowed to commercialize our minds. That is not only the affair of the wage workers; it is the affair of all of us. If one set of our fellow citizens is degraded, you can be absolutely certain that the degradation will spread more or less to all of us. This government is founded on the theory that "all men up" is a safer motto than "some men down." We must make it good.

It is not merely the duty of the wage earner, but it is also the duty of the general public, to see that he has safe and healthy conditions under which to carry on his work. No worker should be compelled, as a condition of earning his daily bread, to risk his life and limb, or be deprived of his health, or have to work under dangerous and bad surroundings. Society owes the worker this because it owes as much to itself. He should not be compelled to make this matter of contract; he ought not to be left to fight alone for decent conditions in this respect. His protection in the place where he works should be guaranteed by the laws of the land. In other words, he should be protected during his working hours against greed and carelessness on the part of unscrupulous employers, just as outside of those working hours both he and his employer are protected in their lives and property against the murderer and the thief.

This opens a vitally important field of legislation to the national government and to the state alike. As Judge Amidon has said, it is humiliating to think how far we of this country are behind most of the other countries in such matters. Practically all civilized countries have for more than a decade prohibited by the strictest regulations the poisonous match industry; yet we had not done anything at all until very recently to protect the laborers against this horrible danger. The national government made an investigation a year ago into this industry, which showed a condition of things unspeakably shocking and revolting. Legislation to prevent these abuses was introduced in Congress, which was not passed. Since then the companies in fault have ostentatiously announced that they have done away with the objectionable conditions. I hope so; but whether they have or not, a law should be passed in stringent form to prevent any possible backsliding.

So it is in the matter of injuries to employees. In what is called "employers' liability" legislation, other countries have accepted the principle that the industry must bear the monetary burden of its human sacrifices, and that the employee who is injured shall have a fixed and definite sum. The United States still proceeds on an outworn and curiously improper principle, in accordance with which it has too often been held by the courts that the frightful burden of the accident shall be borne in its entirety by the very person least able to bear it. Fortunately, in a number of states—in Wisconsin and New York, for instance—these defects in our life are either being remedied, or else being made a subject of intelligent study with a view to their remedy. In New York a bill embodying moderate compensation for accidents has already been passed. Other states will undoubtedly follow in the same path. The Federal Government has, so far as its own employees are concerned, been the first to recognize and put into shape this principle. However, this pioneer law was not made comprehensive enough; it does not cover all the employees of the Federal Government that ought to come within its provisions, and the amount paid for permanent disability or death is entirely inadequate. Nevertheless, it was a great step in advance to have this principle of workingmen's compensation accepted and embodied in the Federal statutes; and the recent action of Congress in providing for a commission to study and report upon the subject gives promise that the same principle will soon be applied to private firms that come within the jurisdiction of the Federal Government.

Women and children should, beyond all question, be protected; and in their cases there can be no question that the government should act. They should be particular objects of our solicitude; and they should be guarded in effective fashion against the demands of a too greedy commercialism. On my recent trip in the neighborhood of Scranton and Wilkes-Barre, every one I spoke to agreed as to the immense improvement that had been wrought by the effective enforcement of the laws prohibiting children under the age of fourteen from working, and prohibiting women from working more than ten hours a day. Personally, I think ten hours a day too long; but, be this as it may, ten hours a day was a great advance.

Among the planks in the platform of the American Federation of Labor, there are some to which I very strongly subscribe. They are:—

1. Free schools; free textbooks; and compulsory education.
2. A workday of not more than eight hours.
3. Release from employment one day in seven.
4. The abolition of the sweatshop system.
5. Sanitary inspection of factory, workshop, mine, and home.
6. Liability of employers for injury to body or loss of life.

(I regard the demand in this form as inadequate. What we need is an automatically fixed compensation for all injuries received by the employee in the course of his duty, this being infinitely better for the employee and more just to the employer. The only sufferers will be lawyers of that undesirable class which exist chiefly by carrying on lawsuits of this nature.)

7. The passage and enforcement of rigid anti-child-labor laws which will cover every portion of this country.

(Similar laws limiting women's labor should be enacted.)

8. Suitable and plentiful playgrounds for children in all the cities.

Inasmuch as prevention is always best, especial attention should be paid to the prevention of industrial accidents by passing laws requiring the use of safety devices. At present the loss of life and limb among the industrial workers of the United States is simply appalling, and every year equals in magnitude the killed and wounded in a fair-sized war. Most of these casualties are preventable; and our legislative policy should be shaped accordingly. It would be a good idea to establish in each city a museum of safety devices, from which the workingmen could get drawings of them and information as to how they could be obtained and used.

The matter of compensation for injuries to employees is, perhaps, more immediately vital than any other. The report of the commission which has begun to look into this matter on behalf of the New York Legislature is well worth reading. The bill presented by the Federation of Labor at Wisconsin on this subject seems excellent. In all dangerous trades the employer should be forced to bear the burden of the accident, so that the shock may not be borne by the community as a whole. This would be a measure of justice in itself, and would do away with a fruitful source of antagonism between employer and employed.

Our ideal should be a rate of wages sufficiently high to enable workmen to live in a manner conformable to American ideals and standards, to educate their children, and to provide for sickness and old age; the abolition of child labor; safety device legislation to prevent industrial accidents; and automatic compensation for losses caused by these industrial accidents.

World Feats

Speech at Omaha
2 SEPTEMBER 1910

I am glad to be with you to-day; and I enjoyed the modest tribute to your worth made by the Senator, and I agree with every word of it.[1] I am particularly pleased to be introduced by the Senator, because he was one of the men upon whom I especially relied while I was President, both while he was in the House and afterwards when he was in the Senate. On one occasion he paid a tribute to me, which may have been entirely unmerited, in which he described what the typical American public servant must be. In my own case all I can say is that I endeavored to live up to that description, and that I was able to accomplish what I did accomplish in Washington only because of the way I was backed up by men like Senator Burkett; and, as we have here to-day a guest from Iowa, let me say also, like Senator Dolliver.[2]

My friends, I come here—back to the West, back to my own people whom I know so well and in whom I believe so deeply because they are such typical Americans. I have returned from a trip abroad, and I think that any one who goes out of this country ought to realize that party lines stop at the water's edge; that in-

---

[1] Senator Elmer Jacob Burkett of Nebraska, a Republican regular who had joined the insurgents on the tariff. Roosevelt had endorsed him for re-election.

[2] Senator Jonathan P. Dolliver of Iowa, one of the leaders of the Republican insurgency.

finitely more important than the questions that divide us one from another within our limits are the great fundamental questions upon which we stand alike without regard to party differences simply as Americans; and that the great feats of which America is proud and the great things which she has done are to be credited to all good Americans.

In traveling in Europe last spring, one thing which especially struck me was the fact that the two feats which made the deepest impression abroad were the cruise of the battle fleet around the world and the digging of the Panama Canal. Wherever I went, wherever I met the great statesmen of foreign nations, I found out that these two feats, among all the feats credited to the American people during the last two decades, had most deeply and favorably affected foreign judgment of our people.

Remember, friends, that foreign judgment of us depends not in the least upon what we say we can do, but upon what we can do. I hate to see an American boast in the presence of a foreigner; it exposes him and his country to laughter. It does no good to boast that we are the greatest nation on the face of the earth; but it does help us when we do a great deed that no other nation has done.

During the past fifteen years we have built up our Navy, and the building up of that Navy has been the most potent means of making the United States respected abroad. Some time after we began to build it up the great military missions abroad sneered and said, "Yes; the Yankees can build ships; but they don't know how to handle them; they cannot do anything with them when they have been built." No nation had ever ventured on the experience of sending a great battle fleet around the world. Other nations have tried it with small squadrons halfway around the world, and they had plenty of difficulties and plenty of failures even with such a small task; but Uncle Sam once for all put an end to this talk about his fleet when he had that fleet undertake a cruise that is to the credit of no other nation under the sun.

Now, there is no use of a nation claiming to be a great nation unless it is prepared to play a great part. A nation such as ours cannot possibly play a great part in international affairs, cannot expect to be treated as a weight in either the Atlantic or the Pacific, or to have its voice as to the Monroe Doctrine, or the management of the Panama Canal, heeded, unless it has a strong and thoroughly efficient Navy. Within the last decade the American Navy has been about trebled in strength and much more than trebled in efficiency, due to its extraordinary progress in marksmanship and maneuvering. And, friends, that Navy is not an affair of the seacoast only. There is not a man who lives in the grass country, in the cattle country, or among the Great Lakes, or alongside the Missouri who is not just as keenly interested in that Navy as if he dwelt on the New England coast, or the Gulf coast, or on Puget Sound. The Navy belongs to all of us. If it wins credit for the nation, it wins for all of us. Now, my friends, more than once in my experience in public life I have found that I got better support from the men in the interior than from the men of the coast when I appealed to them for the upbuilding of the Navy. Take this very instance of sending the battle fleet around the world. As you gentlemen in the Senate and the House remember, there was a great panic along the Atlantic coast when I announced that the fleet was going around the world. It is not a good thing for any one proud of this country to think he has the sole proprietary interest in the fleet or the army or anything else. I wanted to have it understood by ourselves and by foreign powers, not as a menace, but as the strongest kind of provocation to friendliness. That fleet was just as much at home in the Pacific as it was in the Atlantic, and it could go anywhere and would go anywhere when it was necessary. When I announced that it was going around the world, some good people on the Atlantic slope became very much concerned, and some who were a little less good threatened a great outcry, and it was announced that the fleet would not sail. It did sail. Some of my friends of the coordinate branch of the government, as distinguished from the type of friend I have with me to-day, announced that it should not sail because I should not have the money to let it sail; that it should stay where it was,—to which the answer was easy. I said I had the money to send it to the Pacific, and I intended to send it there, and then, if they did not want to appropriate the money to get it back, it was their affair. After this announcement the discussion subsided, except for the conventional and perfunctory remarks that I had been guilty of usurpation of authority. Now, so far from this growth of our Navy representing on our part either a menace of aggression to weaker nations or a menace of war to stronger nations, it has told most powerfully for peace. Everywhere in Europe the cruise of the battle fleet around the world was accepted not only as an extraordinary feat, reflecting the highest honor upon our Navy, but as one of the movements which tended markedly to promote peaceful stability in international relations. No nation regarded the cruise as fraught with any menace of hostility to itself; and yet every nation accepted it as proof that we were not only desirous ourselves to keep the peace, but able to prevent the peace being broken at our expense. No cruise in any way approaching it has ever been made by any fleet of any other power; and the best naval opinion abroad had been that no such feat was possible; that is, that no such cruise as that we actually made could be undertaken by a fleet of such size without innumerable breakdowns and accidents. The best naval people on the other side sneered when I said "The fleet will start"; and they said that the battleships and torpedo boats would be strewed around every part of the globe making repairs. As a matter of fact, the fleet was never, in the whole year and a quarter of its absence in its circumnavigation of the globe, excepting once when there was a typhoon, five minutes late in keeping the schedule time every day, and never did a single vessel fail to put in its appearance at the appointed time of visit. The success of the cruise, performed as it was without a single accident, immeasurably raised the prestige, not only of our fleet, but of our nation; and was a distinct help to the cause of international peace.

As regards the Panama Canal, I really think that outside nations have a juster idea than our own people of the magnitude and success of the work. I wish our people realized what is being done on the Isthmus. If a man of intelligence who had never left the country asked me whether I would advise him to make a short trip to Europe or a trip to the Panama Canal, I would without hesitation advise him to go to the Panama Canal. He would there see in operation the completing of one of the great achievements of modern times. Colonel Goethals, and the men working under him, are rendering a service to this country which can only be paralleled in our past history by some of the services rendered in certain wars. No feat of the kind or of anything like the magnitude has ever been success-fully carried out, and hardly ever been attempted. No other nation has to its credit a task of such magnitude, of such importance, as we will have three years hence when that canal is completed.

Six years ago last spring the American government took possession of the Isthmus. The first two years were devoted to the sanitation of the Isthmus, to assembling the plant and working force, and pro-viding quarters, food, and water supplies. In all these points the success was extraordinary. From one of the plague spots of the globe, one of the most unhealthy regions in the entire world, the Isthmus has been turned into a singularly healthy place of abode, where the death rate is small, and where hundreds of children are now being raised under as favorable conditions as in most parts of the United States. The quarters, food, and water supply are excellent, and the plant the best ever gathered for such a purpose. Active excavation on a large scale did not begin until January, 1907. Three and a half years have gone by since then, and three-fifths of the total excavation has already been accomplished. I had no idea that such a rate of progress was possible. Our people are really not awake to the fact that such a rate has obtained. The amount taken out has passed anything which previous experience warranted us in believing to be possible. In 1908 and 1909 the monthly average of rock and earth removed was three million yards, notwithstanding the fact that nine months of each year constituted a season of very heavy rainfall.

There remains to be excavated only about sixty million cubic yards. If we could keep up the past average of excavation, this should be done in twenty months; but it is impossible to maintain such a ratio as the depth increases, for the output necessarily diminishes as the field of operation narrows. Still, it is certain that such a rate can be maintained as will enable the workers to finish the excavation considerably in advance of the date fixed for the opening of the canal, January 1, 1915. When I announced on the authority of the experts that the canal would be opened on New Year's Day, 1915, even the friends of the canal said, "Ah! of course, it is very nice to say so; but these things are never done as quickly as people hope; and it will be some years after." Well, instead of being some time after the date fixed, it will be some time before the date fixed. I believe that the canal will be opened from six months to a year before.

The work has two great features: the Culebra Cut, which I have been considering; and the great dam at Gatum. The latter is to imprison the waters of the Chagres and other streams into a lake with an area of one hundred and sixty-four square miles. This work is advancing steadily, and just as successfully as the work on the Culebra Cut. The water which is ultimately to fill the lock is now flowing through the concrete spillway in the center of the dam, the Chagres having been diverted from its bed and placed under complete control. The construction of the dam has advanced sufficiently to convince the engineers in charge of the work of its absolute stability and imperviousness. The concrete work on the lock is advancing so rapidly that the first double-set at Gatun will be completed this coming November, and the engineer in charge has announced that all the concrete in all the locks will be in place two years hence. The date of final completion and formal opening of the canal to the commerce of the world will be determined by the time consumed in placing one great steel gate, emergency dams, and all appliances for operating the docks. But those in charge of the work announce without hesitation that everything will be finished well in advance of January 1, 1915.

This is a stupendous record of achievement. As a people, we are rather fond of criticizing ourselves, and sometimes with very great justice; but even the most pessimistic critic should sometimes think of what is to our credit. Among our assets of the past ten years will be placed the extraordinary ability, integrity, and success with which we have handled all the problems inherited as the result of the Spanish War; the way we have handled ourselves in the Philippines, in Cuba, in Porto Rico, in San Domingo, and in Panama. The cruise of the battle fleet around the world was a striking proof that we had made good with the Navy; and what we have done at Panama represents the accomplishment of one of the great feats of the ages. It is a feat which reflects the highest honor upon our country; and our gratitude is due to every man who has taken an honorable part in any capacity in bringing about its performance.

So far, I have been speaking of what we have done, and you have applauded it. It is very interesting to tell what we have done; but that is not the important thing. The important thing is to do the next job well. We have now a further duty to perform in connection with the canal, and that is fortifying it. We took that canal upon the ground that Uncle Sam was big enough to tackle the job, and now we have got to show that Uncle Sam is big enough to make a good job of it. We are in honor bound to fortify it ourselves, and only by so doing can we effectively guarantee its neutrality; and, moreover, effectively guarantee that it shall not be used against us. I want the good will of every nation; I want to deserve it; but in vital matters I do not want to trust to it. The good will is felt immensely if we have a first-class Navy and adequate fortifications; but nothing will help us keep in a state of profound peace more than a knowledge that our men can shoot straight, and will, if they have to. The chief material advantage—certainly one of the chief material advantages—which we shall gain by the canal's construction is the way in which it will, for defensive purposes, double the power of the United States Navy. We must either have a Navy so big that we shall be able to put half in the Atlantic and half in the Pacific, or must be able to put into either ocean a Navy of the present size. It is not a blunder, but a crime, to divide the present Navy between the two. We must either double it, or we must be able to transfer our fleet from the Pacific to the Atlantic when we need it. That can be done only through a canal.

To refuse to fortify the canal, and, above all, to consider for a moment such an act of utter weakness and folly as to invite other nations to step in and guarantee the neutrality of this purely American work (and thereby really to make it certain that, in the event of war, we should find the canal used against us, as our fleets would be forbidden to pass through it, or else our opponent's fleets permitted to) would be to incur, and quite rightfully, the contempt of the world.[3] It would mean the complete abandonment of the Monroe Doctrine; it would be a wicked blow to our prestige in the Pacific; and, moreover, it would be in its essence treason to the destiny of this republic. We built that canal ourselves, and we do not have to have anybody else to come in and say how it shall be used. If it was not our intention to have our sayso in the management of that canal, we had no business to undertake it, or to go into the expenditure of the scores of millions involved. It is not an act showing a peaceful disposition to ask other nations to come in and do all that we ought to do. I want Uncle Sam to be peaceful; I want Uncle Sam to show scrupulous regard for the rights of others; but I want to see Uncle Sam owe his safety to two facts: in the first place, that he will do nothing but good to men; and, in the second place, that he will submit to wrong from no man. Therefore, I am glad we have an efficient fleet; therefore, I am glad that we have completed in such splendid and successful fashion the Panama Canal; and, therefore, I say that unless, as a people, we intend to occupy a contempti-

[3] British publications like the *London Daily News* and the *Westminster Gazette* denounced Roosevelt for his remarks on the Panama Canal in this address. Roosevelt contended that the Hay-Pauncefote Treaty between the United States and Great Britain, ratified in 1902, while it reaffirmed the principle of the neutralization of an isthmian canal, recognized, by implication, the right of the United States to fortify the canal since it did not specifically forbid such action.

ble attitude, we will fortify and police and defend that canal ourselves, and see that it is used impartially by all the nations of the
earth, and at the same time see that no nation shall use it against
our own interests.

PART TWO

The Old Moralities

The Crook

Speech at Kansas City
1 SEPTEMBER 1910

Mr. Chairman, I thank you for the more than kind words
that you have said.[1] I disagree with some of them. The American
people owe nothing to the man whom they have honored by making
him President compared to what that man owes to the American
people. I am most deeply sensible of what I owe to the people of the
United States, and I shall try to carry myself as, in my opinion, every
man who has been President should carry himself—as a man bound
in every action of his private life to try to justify the faith that the
people reposed in him. I particularly appreciate what the Chairman
said when he said that I had always put patriotism above party. In
my judgment, no man is a good American who is not, of course, an
American first—an American before he is a member of any section
of the American people such as a party or a class. I hold that the
only real service which a party man can render his party is to make
that party more responsive to the needs of the American people.

There are certain matters which should never be treated
as party matters; and foremost among these is the great and vital

[1] In Kansas City, somewhat to his discomfort, Roosevelt was hailed as an
insurgent. He spoke to 18,000 cheering people in the Kansas City auditorium.
President William T. Bland of the Kansas City Commercial Club, who introduced him, declared: "It was Roosevelt who awakened the public conscience
which had already slept too long."

121

virtue of honesty. Honesty should be treated as a prime necessity to our success as a nation. The minute that a question of honesty as against dishonesty is involved, then we must all act together as Americans, without the slightest regard to party affiliations. I do not care who a thief is; I regard him as a thief and not as a party man. The first man to attack a scoundrel in any party should be the man of that party. The Chairman was kind enough to say that I had acted up to my words; that I had not preached what I had not at least tried to practice while in office. I certainly did try always to proceed upon the theory that there would be no need of my political opponents raising the cry of "Turn the rascals out," for I would turn them out myself. With the invaluable aid of Senator Bristow here, I turned the rascals out of the Post Office Department;[2] and we discriminated just to this extent between any Republican and any Democrat: we gave the precedence to the Republican in pitching him out.

And as we dealt with the crooked public official, so we dealt with the crooked private citizen. If satisfactory evidence was brought before me in my capacity as President, I had the Attorney-General of the United States to proceed against the highest politician, whether it was a Republican Senator in Oregon or in Kansas or a Democratic Governor in Oklahoma. And I will add, gentlemen, that the unfavorable opinions entertained of me by the Senators, Governors, and other people in question I have always considered as a tribute. I think I value the ill will of those men almost as much as I value the good will of the honest Senators, the honest Governors, and honest public men with whom it has been my great privilege to work for the welfare of the people. We gave the same justice to the big man and to the little man, to the rich and to the poor man.

[2] Senator Joseph L. Bristow of Kansas. In 1897, President McKinley named Bristow Fourth Assistant Postmaster-General. In the McKinley administration, postal investigations revealed corruption in the Cuban postal services; the responsible officials were sent to the penitentiary. In 1903, President Roosevelt ordered a probe of the United States Post Office Department. Employing fifty trained inspectors, the investigation was perhaps the most thorough ever conducted by the federal government.

We never attacked a man because he was a man of one political faith or another, because he did or did not possess wealth; and we never shielded him because he was poor or rich, because he belonged to any particular church or to any particular party. But I also wish you especially to remember that we never hesitated to shield him and stand up for him once we were convinced that he was improperly attacked. There is no greater foe of honesty—no more evil enemy of honesty—than the man who, for any reason, in any capacity, attacks, or seeks to attack, an honest man for a crime which he has not committed. Falsely accusing an honest man of dishonesty is an act which stands on the same level of infamy with that of the dishonest man himself; and it is no higher duty to attack the dishonest man than it is to exonerate the honest man falsely accused; and I should be ashamed to hesitate the fraction of a second longer in one case than in the other.

Remember that honesty cannot be unilateral. Good citizens should cordially distrust the man who can never see dishonesty excepting in men of the class he dislikes. The reckless agitator who invariably singles out men of wealth as furnishing the only examples of dishonesty; the equally unscrupulous—but no more unscrupulous —reactionary who can see dishonesty only in a blackmailing politician or a crooked labor leader; both stand on the same plane of obnoxiousness. You will never get honesty from politicians until you exact honesty from business men; on the other hand, you brand yourselves as fools or as hypocrites if you say that the corporation owner, or the employer, is always the dishonest man, and the poor man never; that it is only the wealthy man who corrupts the politician and never the politician who blackmails the corporation.

Any man in his senses knows that there are plenty of corporations in this country that prosper by bribing legislators just as they prosper by swindling the public; and any man in his senses ought to know, in addition, that there are plenty of corrupt men of small means who, in legislative or other bodies, try to blackmail corporations, and try to blackmail other people as well. If they doubt this, let them look at the revelations of corruption in my own state—New York—and in yours, my hearers—here in Missouri; let them look at what has occurred in California and what has occurred in Illinois.[3] In Illinois, for instance, one of the rascalities developed by the recent investigation was the existence of a combination of legislators who blackmailed, not only wealthy corporations, but poor fishermen along a certain river, forcing them to pay to prevent legislation which would have interfered with their business. Remember that the reason in each case why a man committed a given crooked act is usually to be found in the fact that he was a scoundrel; it was not because he happened to blackmail a rich man or a poor man, but because he was crooked and he blackmailed the first man that came handy; and you help him if you confine your denunciations of dishonesty to include only the men of one class. Distrust men who would teach you to hate only men of wealth who go wrong; distrust equally the man, judge, newspaper writer, or wealthy private citizen, who cannot see wrong if it is committed by the big business men with whom he associates. Above all, distrust the man who ever seeks to get you to support him on the ground that he will do something wrong in your interest.

Now, scoundrels who do these kinds of things are, of course, the very men who, on the one hand, will blackmail a corporation if they get a chance, and, on the other hand, will cheerfully, if the chance occurs, sell themselves to the corporation against the interests of the public. Their corruption is no more due to the action of the corporation than the corruption of the corporation is due to their action; and evil, and not good, is done by the honest but misguided man who would persuade you that either fact is true. Our duty is to war with equal sternness against the corrupt man of great wealth

[3] A series of investigations in New York had revealed the practice of introducing "strike" bills to mulct corporations. The noted reformer, Joseph W. Folk, had exposed corruption in Missouri. An investigation in San Francisco had led to the trial of Abraham Ruef and others for corrupt dealings in the Bay area. Concern about graft in Illinois had reached a peak with the probe of corruption in connection with the election of William Lorimer to the United States Senate.

and the small man who makes a trade of corruption; our fight is against both the swindling corporation and the blackmailing or bribe-taking politician. The politician who whines that he is corrupted by a big corporation and would have been good enough if the corporation had let him alone may safely be put down as a man whose virtue was so frail that it was not worth preserving.

We cannot afford to limit a campaign against corruption to those who happen to have a certain social status. We need laws which shall put the corporation out of business so far as concerns corrupting the servants of the public and betraying the rights of the public. I believe that the great issue now before the public is the doing away with special privilege in all its forms; doing away with the power of the big corporation to control legislation in its interests and to interfere in politics in order to secure privileges to which it is not entitled. But I regard the essential factor in this campaign as being an aroused civic conscience which will unsparingly condemn dishonesty in every form and in every man, high or low. It is not the man who inveighs only against corruption as seen in men of wealth who hopes to end all corruption on the part of men of wealth. It is the man who insists on honesty, who strives to bring about a condition when honesty shall be accepted as a matter of course throughout our nation, and when the conscience of the community—the popular spirit in the community—will not tolerate any man who is a crooked man or a dishonest man. The reckless would-be reformer or reckless demagogue who, in speaking or writing, seeks to persuade us that we need pay heed to corruption only when it shows itself in the rich man, is doing as great a moral wrong as the rich man whose low moral standard tends to lower the social standard of the whole community. The people of this country will get justice from the corporations only if they both do justice to them and rigidly exact it from them. Unless they do justice to rich men, they put a premium upon injustice and dishonesty among rich men. Let us hold them to the strictest accountability for any wrongdoing; but let us insist upon honesty in our own ranks no less than in theirs. Let us war on crookedness of every kind in the man of small means as well as the man of large means, and in the man of large means exactly as in the man of small means. Let us judge each man by his conduct and not by his social or financial condition.

My friends, you applaud these sentiments; you could not do otherwise. It is a good thing to applaud them; but the necessary thing is to go back to your own homes and in your daily lives to live up to them. Words are of no consequence whatever except as they are realized in deeds. The promise of a candidate is worse than worthless if it is not made good by his actions if he is elected. A liar on the stump is, if anything, just a shade worse than the liar off the stump; and, on the other hand, if you come to public meetings to indulge in the luxury of applauding fine sentiments which you forget as soon as you leave the building, then all you have done is to weaken a little the spring of your own conscience. If I were asked to name the three faults against which we of this free republic should most unrelentingly war, I should name dishonesty, lawless violence, and, in the third place, untruthfulness and mendacity— especially mendacity which takes the form of slander. I have been in politics for thirty years. For thirty years I have striven, so far as the power was given me, to fight for the cause of decency; and I feel that the greatest drawback in any such struggle is the man who consistently speaks what is not true until he misleads the public, so that they cannot tell the true from the false. I do not care whether that man is a politician in the campaign or a writer in a magazine or in the public press. The very reason that makes it essential that we should point out corruption and misconduct where they exist also makes it essential that we should not lie by saying that they exist where they do not exist. The man that falsely accuses a public servant, who is honest, of dishonesty, is bringing joy to the heart of every crooked man. Nothing so pleases the dis- honest man in public life as to have an honest man falsely accused, for the result of innumerable accusations finally is to produce a habit of mind in the public which accepts each accusation as having something true in it and none as being all true; so that, finally, they believe that the honest man is a little crooked and that the crooked man is not much more dishonest than the rest. The enormous power of the writers of the country in the public press and in the magazines alike is such that those wielding it should feel that their responsibility is as great as that of the public servants themselves.

If, day after day, you read what is not true, it becomes finally impossible for you to tell what is black from what is white; and you look upon all men, good and bad, alike. The liar is as bad as the thief; and he is the right-hand support of the thief. I think that the very highest duty that can be performed by any man who writes is to point out corruption fearlessly and expose all that is crooked —all that is evil; and only less high, and less high by the merest shade, is his duty to speak the truth only and never to accuse an honest man of dishonesty. I do not ask it on behalf of the honest man; I ask it on behalf of the public who by such accusations are robbed of the power of discrimination. In the long run the honest man's reputation will take care of itself. It is not for him, but it is for the people at large who are so puzzled by seeing every man, whether he is honest or not, attacked in the same fashion, that they come to regard all accusations as, on the whole, false, and all men accused as having done something that warrants accusation.

And, my friends, so of lawless violence. I have said that I would strive to punish equally the rich and the poor man who does wrong. I would go a bit further, and would punish the rich man a little more, because he has had better opportunities. But be equally stern in dealing with crimes of violence. Do you realize the danger that this country is in from corruption, and do you realize the danger also that comes from lawless violence? Take the working-men, the laboring men. I will do everything in my power for them except what is wrong, and that I would do neither for them nor for any one else. In time of civil disorder, when laws are set at naught and mob violence rules, the first duty of every honest and upright civil official is to restore order. All question of reform must wait until order is restored. While the mob rules there is no time to find out the right and the wrong of the question at issue between that mob and any person or any corporation. No civilization can exist unless the laws are enforced in due and orderly fashion, and the corrupt man who, with his wealth, plunders his neighbors and corrupts the representatives of the people is no worse than the man who in any way incites his fellow men to violence and murder.

I have just come from a trip to Africa, and I had a very good time there. Afterwards I passed through Europe, and I came back thinking well of the countries I had visited, with friendly feelings for them; but, O my countrymen, I came back thinking more strongly than ever before that, in spite of all our shortcomings, and in spite of all the things that we have left undone and ought to have done, nowhere on the earth does the average man or the average woman have such a chance to get the best possible out of life as here in our own land. Now, I would not for one moment blind myself to the need of hard work to drive out what is evil in our own country. Let us face the evil boldly, and do our best to overcome it. Do not, however, let us make the mistake of shutting our eyes to the good. On the whole, in this great democracy of the West, in this great republic which stands on a continent, which grasps the ocean on either side, popular rights are better guarded than anywhere else, and the average man is given a better chance than anywere else. My friends, be proud of that fact, and realize the responsibility that accompanies it.

I was struck by two things especially while traveling abroad. One was that in every country I visited the name of America is the symbol of golden hope for the people of other lands. The man with whom life has gone hard,—the man who feels that fate is against him, the man who, do what he can, is unable to succeed as he is entitled to succeed,—looks longingly to this land as the land which contains the promise for men like him. But, my friends, there was another and sadder side; there was something else. The news of every crime of corruption, every crime of lawless violence, committed here in the United States is sent abroad. The news goes abroad to sadden the hearts of those who hope for the success of popular government, and is cause for sardonic mirth to every reactionary who desires to see the great democratic experiment of government by and for the people fail here in the West. Every time that there is an act of flagrant corruption here in the United States, or deed of lawless violence by a mob, or corruption in public life or business life, every time a murderer is acquitted by a jury when he ought to have been convicted, every time a rich malefactor is let off on a technicality, or otherwise there is a failure to secure justice in any case—every time that such things occur the heart of every opponent of free government is gladdened, and the heart of every man who hopes for the regeneration of humanity through the application of democratic principles to-day is saddened. I do not suppose that if we refuse to do what is right for our own sakes we can be expected to do what is right for the sake of others. Yet I believe that you ought to feel a burden of obligation resting upon you, not only because you are the citizens of this republic, but because each of you is, in a measure, the custodian of the hope of the world. If we fail here, if we in America fail in our great experiment of self-government, woe to us, and woe also to all the nations of the earth, whom we will forever rob of the brightest hope that they now have. I ask of you men and women here—I ask that, in your private and in your public lives, you carry yourselves as you should carry yourselves—you, the men and women upon whose shoulders rests the proud fabric of the greatest republic upon which the sun has ever shone. I ask that you do this for your own sakes; I ask more earnestly that you do it for the sake of the children who are to come after you, for the children who are to inherit this our land

and have a right to ask that they receive it from us as we received it from our fathers; that we shall pass it on to them intact; and I ask this not only for the sake of your own children, but for the sake of the world, so that America shall always stand as the symbol of golden hope to the nations of mankind.

The Public Press

Speech at the Milwaukee Auditorium
7 SEPTEMBER 1910

Before I come down to the subject of my speech I wish to say a word about the trade schools—the municipal trade school which I visited this morning. When I received the invitation from the Milwaukee Press Club while I was in mid-Africa, I accepted it promptly. I wished to come here to your city, and I was particularly glad to come as the guest of your Club, and I soon afterwards made the stipulation that I should be taken to see your municipal schools for boys and girls. I wish it had been in my power to do more than a fraction of the other things that the very good people who are my hosts wanted me to do, but it was simply a physical impossibility. In every city that I have visited, my hosts, in the very nicest and kindliest spirit, have proceeded to see that I did not suffer one minute from physical stagnation, and they have also proceeded upon the assumption that I could be happy only if I were given not one minute to myself. I wish to say that while all did their duty in that respect, I think my hosts of Milwaukee gave me a larger program than anywhere I have yet visited.

I wanted to see the trade schools because I regard you as having taken here in Milwaukee an all-important first step in incorporating these trade schools into your common-school system. Our republic has no justification unless it is a genuine democracy

—a democracy economically as well as politically—a democracy in which there is a really sincere effort to realize the ideal of equality of opportunity for all men. And there can be no such equality of opportunity if a man is either helped by special privilege or hampered by the special privileges which others have. Now, one way to secure such equality of opportunity is, so far as possible, to give equality of start. In other words, give the full-grown man, the full-grown woman, who starts in life to make his or her way according to the abilities given to him or her, as good a chance as we are able to give them. That means that it is our duty to provide such means of education as will enable each man to become a self-respecting unit in the community. If there is a large class of people who, because good chances are denied to them, live under intolerable and harsh conditions, and are beaten down and degraded by the forces against which they contend—if there exists such a large class, it is not only a bad thing for them, but it is a bad thing for all of us. It might as well be accepted as axiomatic that in the long run, speaking generally, we are going to go up or down together. And if there is a large class of people who undeservedly find conditions intolerable, it will be bad for the whole republic. Now, mind you, I said undeservedly. There always will be, as long as mankind continues as it is at the present time, in every community a certain number of people who do not perform their duty because they do not try. Now, I have nothing to say in behalf of them. The individual who is naturally vicious, naturally lazy, and is a man of jealous disposition, or a man of arrogant disposition, I am not pleading for; and I have a hearty contempt for those who try to excuse his shortcomings upon the plea of bad social conditions. If a man is lazy, if he is vicious, if he will not do his whole work, I am very sorry for his wife and children; but I am not in the least sorry for him. There are too many people who have a right to sympathy for me to waste it upon those who have not the right to it. I not only have sympathy for those who are oppressed through no fault of theirs, but I believe that we should do all that we can do for them.

Now, the trade schools here mark the beginning of an effort to fit each man to do the very best that lies in him in the world. There is not a surplusage here, or anywhere, of the highly skilled man who can do his particular job in the best possible manner; there is always a demand for him in any walk of life. When you get our average laboring man—our average wage worker—turned out of school that kind of man, you will have gone a long way towards solving some of the most difficult questions with which this republic has to deal. Well, that is just what I find you are doing here with the few people—there are only very few—whom you are turning out of these industrial schools. The boy is not taken in until he is about sixteen or eighteen. He must have gone through a certain amount in the public schools; he must be able to read and write English; to do a certain amount of arithmetic; he must have reached about the eighth grade in the grammar school. Many I found had been but one or two years in the high schools. Then he is put into this school,—this trade school,—and then he graduates at twenty or twenty-one, and he is able to get a job at once. He is trained during those two years to become a skilled workman, and, as a by-product to that industrial school training, he unquestionably tends to become a good citizen; he is pretty apt to be a decent, law-abiding, self-respecting member of the community.

There is another thing. I am sure that we have all now awakened to the fact that it is not well to have a system of education which tends to educate people away from their life work; and it is a very bad thing to have a system of education which makes men look down on skilled and trained muscular exertion—the skilled and trained work of the body. Too often the son of the skilled mechanic, the blacksmith, the carpenter, feels that he is rising if he becomes a third-rate clerk. Now, that is a very unfortunate condition of things. We ought to do our best to see that reward and respect come in greater proportion than at present to the man who does the best form of manual labor. Personally, it has never been any effort to me to give that respect, because I could not help giving it. I have always felt a very real regard, a very real respect, for the man who works at a handicraft with such skill as to show mastery of his muscles. I cannot imagine a finer type of citizen than the average engineer, fireman, or trainman generally on the railroads. I have prized many honors I have received, but there has been no honor that I have prized more than being elected an honorary member of the Locomotive Firemen's Brotherhood; and I prize it because those men have the qualities that I would like to have and that I admire in men. The smith, the carpenter, the skilled mechanic of any kind is as much entitled to respect as any man who succeeds in any other profession; and by giving him special training in these special schools—a special training which will bring a special reward—you are doing your part to restore the equilibrium of regard in which the professions and trades should be held in the community.

I was almost more interested in the girls' school than in the boys', because, important though it is to have good men in a community, it is even more important to have good women; and while I believe that the normal end striven for by every man and woman alike should be a happy family life,—the life of husband and wife, father and mother,—and therefore that woman's training should be primarily for home work, yet, as girls under modern conditions so often have to go into industry, it is most important that if they do go into it they should go properly equipped. It is bad for a man to have to take employment at less than a living wage—at less than a wage that will enable him to support himself as a self-respecting man; but it is worse for a girl to have to take such employment, for she is exposed to dangers to which the man is not. These schools turn out girls sufficiently trained to enable them to get reasonable remuneration—a remuneration which will enable them to live decently, and remove them from the pitiable condition of being untrained girls competing with multitudes of other untrained girls for an insufficient number of places which, if obtained, yield a wage insufficient to enable the girl to live.

I believe that the workingmen and workingwomen of Milwaukee ought to realize what chances these schools open to their children, —to the boys, and, above all, to the girls,—and ought to take advantage of them.

And now, my friends, I come to what I have especially to say this evening. The Press Club having sent all the way to Africa to ask me to speak to them, I am going to repay them with gross ingratitude by speaking with frankness about their profession.

In our country I am inclined to think that almost, if not quite, the most important profession is that of the newspaper man, including the man of the magazines, especially the cheap magazines, and the weeklies; and I speak as a member of the brotherhood myself.[1] The newspaper men—publishers, editors, reporters—are just as much public servants as are the men in the government service themselves, whether those men be elected or appointed officers. Now, we have always held in higher honor the public man who did his duty, and we have always felt that the public man who did not do his duty was deserving of a peculiar degree of reprobation. And just the same way about the newspaper man. The editor, the publisher, the reporter, who honestly and truthfully puts the exact facts before the public, who does not omit for improper reasons things that ought to be stated, who does not say what is not true, who does not color his facts so as to give false impressions, who does not manufacture his facts, who really is ready, in the first place, to find out what the truth is, and, in the next place, to state it accurately—that man occupies one of the most honorable positions in the community. A number of years ago I knew a citizen of Milwaukee who was just such a man as I have described, and who was, I felt, not only one of the most useful citizens of Milwaukee, but one of the most useful citizens of the United States—Horace Rublee.[2] Now, it is open to

[1] Roosevelt was contributing editor to the *Outlook*.
[2] Horace Rublee (1829-1896), who began newspaper work in 1852, was a founder of the Republican Party and served as Minister to Switzerland. As editor of the *Milwaukee Sentinel* from 1883 to 1896, he was one of America's best-known editors, and his editorials were widely quoted and reprinted.

any man to disagree with Horace Rublee on public questions. It is perfectly possible that if he had lived to the present day, he and I might not have agreed on all public questions; but he was a man of such transparent uprightness and honesty, of such vehement scorn of what was corrupt and untrue, of a virtue so nice, so sensitive, that the mere thought of corruption could not enter into any human being's mind in thinking of him. He was so fearless—as fearless of the mob as of the corrupt corporation—that whatever the differences of your political opinion, you could not but respect him; you could not but feel that he was a very real asset of value in the community. Now, you compare the attitude of the man whom I have just named with the attitude of certain other men, whom I shall not name, and whose reputation and character are such that any man who works for them, or for whom they work, always, when he finds himself in decent society, mentions his occupation with either defiance or apology.

Power always brings with it responsibility. You cannot have power to work well without having so much power as to be able to work ill, if you turn yourselves that way. The very fact that a newspaper has a great power for good means that it has also a great power for evil. I do not think that is enough. I will go further. I think that it is not enough for a newspaper man to make up his mind that he won't use the paper to debauch the public conscience; if he is neutral about good and bad and makes his profession, so far as he is able, neutral in doing good and evil, it simply becomes a profession for which you have not much use in the way of blame and not much more use in the way of praise. He must have high ideals, and he must be able to get those ideals adopted by a reasonable proportion of his fellows, if the profession is to rank as high as it ought to.

A few years ago, at a meeting of newspaper men in New York, there was a speech made, and, I am sorry to say, greeted with applause, which always seemed to me to explain the degradation of a portion of the press. The speaker was connected in a high position with one of the papers of great circulation, and in addressing his fellow newspaper men, said, in effect (I cannot pretend to quote his exact words), that it was nonsense to talk about a newspaper having a mission, whether to do good or to advance reforms; that the newspaper business was to sell as many copies of the paper as possible, and that meant giving the public anything the public wanted; and if it wanted what was not good, then that was the affair of the public and not the affair of the paper. The sentiment was applauded by a good many of those present, and I am sorry to say that the applause of many of them was sincere, to judge by the way their papers have since acted. The speaker said the newspaper business was like any other business; like that of storekeepers who tried to give their customers what they wanted; that the newspaper should do the same thing. In the first place, he was wrong. A storekeeper who now tried to give his customers everything they wanted in the way of food would be speedily arrested under the pure food law; and there would be any number of customers who, after their wants were gratified, would find that they came under the exercise of the police power of the state. So, then, from even the lowest standpoint that newspaper man was wrong. He was not endeavoring to put the newspaper business on the level of other businesses; he was trying to put it below other businesses.

Now, the highest type of newspaper man ought to try to put his business above all other businesses. The editor, who stands as a judge in a community, should be one of the men to whom you would expect to look up, because his function as an editor makes him a more important man than the average merchant, the average business man, the average professional man can be. He wields great influence; and he cannot escape the responsibility of wielding it. If he wields it well, honor is his beyond the honor that comes to the average man who does well; if he wields it ill, shame should be his beyond the shame that comes to the average man who does ill; and what I say of the editor applies to every man who writes for a newspaper or a magazine, or who is connected with it in any capacity. If he is a good citizen, he will take a pride in his work that will make him feel that he must try to make it one of the best types of work done by any man in the whole community. If he is not the right type of man, then he is mischievous just in proportion as he has power to do good.

Exactly as I put as the first requisite of the man in public life that he should be honest, so I put as the first requisite of the man writing for the newspaper that he should tell the truth. Now, it is important that he should tell the whole truth, for there can be no greater service rendered than the exposure of corruption in either public life or in business, or in that intricate web of public life and business which exists too often in America to-day. I cannot say with sufficient emphasis how earnestly I hope that corruption will be exposed wherever found, and that a man ought to be especially anxious to expose it in his own class or in his own party. I will draw no distinction between corrupt men of my own party and those of the opposite party, excepting that I will be just a trifle more anxious to get at those of my own party, because I feel a little more responsible for it.

If an article is published in a magazine, exposing corruption, and the article tells the truth, I do not care what it is, the writer has rendered the greatest possible service by writing it; but I want to be certain that he is telling the truth, and if he does not tell the truth he does wrong in more than one way. It is not only that he wrongs one individual; he wrongs the public, because he deprives them of the chance to discriminate between honest men and scoundrels. The greatest service that can be rendered to the scoundrel in public life is to attack the honest man untruthfully. If the honest man is lied about, either the lies are believed, and he and the scoundrel are put on the same plane of scoundrelism, or else the lies themselves tend to produce the impression in the public mind that no statements about public men are true, and that, therefore, the truth when told about corrupt men in public life can be disregarded also. Incessant falsehood inevitably produces in the public mind a certain disbelief in good men and a considerable disbelief in the charges against bad men; so that there results the belief that there are no men entirely good and no men entirely bad, and that they are all about alike and colored gray. Now, that is the worst possible frame of mind that can be induced in a democracy like ours. It is essential that the public should know the character of its servants; and it is essential that the public should not be misled into believing a dishonest public servant honest and an honest public servant dishonest. Those who mislead them are doing as much damage as the dishonest men themselves. Mark Twain, who was not only a great humorist, but a great philosopher, in his proverbs by Pudd'nhead Wilson, said that there are eight hundred and sixty-nine different kinds of lies, but that the only one authoritatively prohibited is bearing false witness against your neighbor. The politician —I am a politician—and the writer for periodicals or the press— and I am one again—should bear steadily in mind that the eighth and ninth commandments are equally binding: "Thou shalt not steal; Thou shalt not bear false witness against thy neighbor." So much for the newspaper men, my friends.

Now, speaking for all of us, we have much to do to make this republic a better place to live in, to secure a better standard of justice and fair dealing between man and man in it. Much can be done by legislation and much by honest administration of the law. Do not understand me as minimizing that. There are many laws, many schemes of legislation, which I want to see put on the statute books of both nation and state. There is much that I desire to see done in the direction of doing away with special privileges and divorcing corrupt business from political activities, in the direction of securing a better chance for each man to show the stuff that is in him. I realize to the full the importance of what can be done by all of us acting collectively,—through the government,—but after all, when all has been said and done, the thing that is most important is for each of us to apply, in his or her way, the old humdrum, workaday virtues; and as regards those, I know quite well that preaching does not amount to anything unless the preaching is transmuted into practice. Your opinions depend at least as much on your actions as your actions upon your opinions. You fathers and mothers in the audience well know that if you get your children to behave in a certain fashion so that they always do tell the truth, they will formulate the theory that it is always right to tell the truth; that their actions will influence their opinions rather than their opinions their actions.

I remember a young fellow who came to me for a little advice. He said he felt timid about horses and asked how he could get over the timidity, and I told him, by acting as if he were not timid. It took him some time to realize that the only way to get rid of the wrong sensation was to perform the act as if he were enjoying the right sensation. He did not make himself act as a brave man because he was not afraid, but finally ceased to be afraid because he acted like a brave man. Now, I want you to do the same way in citizenship. It is a fine thing to come to a public meeting like this; but it is not doing you or me a mite of good if I speak insincerely and you merely listen and applaud and don't do anything else after you get to your homes. If I preach to you what I do not try to live up to myself, I am a despicable character, and you have no business to listen to me; and if you find yourselves applauding sentiments of justice and righteousness, and then go back home and encourage and connive at dishonesty or mendacity, then the right stuff is not in you. The only value of words uttered or listened to comes when they are transmuted into deeds.

I believe in the future of this republic, and I believe in it primarily because I believe that, more and more, our citizens are waking up to the need of making practice conform to profession, and are declining to listen to spread-eagle heroics, which they accept merely as intellectual efforts divorced from all practical application, and are insisting that the conduct of their representatives and leaders shall measurably conform to the standards which they have in the abstract accepted as desirable. I don't want you to put your ideals so high that you feel that there is no use in trying to live up to them, because you cannot do it. I don't want you to show that kind of citizenship which thinks that a conscientious announcement on Sunday that one is a sinner condones active participation in sin the other six days.

In a democracy like ours we cannot expect the stream to rise higher than its source. If the average man and the average woman are not of the right type, your public men will not be of the right type. The average man must be a decent man in his own home, he must pull his own weight, he must be a decent neighbor, and a man with whom you like to work and with whom you like to deal, or he cannot be a good citizen. That is good as a beginning; but it is not enough. He must show in his relations with his fellows and in his dealing with the state the essentials of good citizenship. Genius is not necessary. Genius is a fine thing; but fortunately character is not only more common, but better. What he needs to show is character, and there are three essential qualities going to make up character.

In the first place, there is honesty. The bolder a man is the worse he is, if he hasn't honesty. Don't be misled by that unfortunate trait sometimes shown by our people—the trait of deifying mere smartness, meaning thereby mental subtlety and ability unencumbered by any sense of responsibility.

But honesty is not enough. I don't care how honest a man is, if he is timid he is no good. I don't want to see a division of our citizenship into good men who are afraid and bad men who are not at all afraid. The honest man who is afraid is of just as little use in civic life as in war.

You need honesty and then you need courage; but both of them together are not enough. I don't care how honest a man is and how brave he is; if he is a natural-born fool you can do nothing with him; and perhaps this applies particularly to people in the profession of politics. Of course, the bolder a politician is, if he is dishonest, the worse he is, hunt him out of public life; and a feeble, well-meaning, timid politician, like the other good, timid people, is of no use; but the bold, incorruptible politician who stupidly goes wrong may be just as useless to a community in the long run as if he were hired by some dishonest man to do his work. So there is a third quality; that is, you must possess the saving grace of common sense.

When you get into your average citizen honesty,—militant not merely passive honesty,—courage, and common sense, you will find that your representatives in public life will soon show the same traits; and when they do, we shall have gone a long way toward solving the questions which must be solved and must be solved aright, if this nation is to be, as it shall and will be, not merely the greatest republic upon which the sun has ever shone, but the nation which holds out the lamp of hope to all the other nations throughout the world.

The Good Citizen

Speech at Pueblo
30 AUGUST 1910

In Colorado Springs, some years ago, I laid the foundation stone of a Young Men's Christian Association building. I am particularly glad to have the chance of doing so here, where the Chairman,[1] the man chiefly concerned in the erection of the building, is himself a veteran of the great war, because I believe in the two qualities of manliness and decency. I don't care a rap for the good man who cannot do anything good because he is timid; and as for the efficient scoundrel, the more efficient he is, the more I wish to hunt him out of politics or business. The Young Men's Christian Association stands for decency, for the man who does well in his family and in his home life, and as a neighbor and with reference to the state and the nation; and it also stands for the manly virtues. Your Chairman, the head of this Young Men's Christian Association, lost an arm in battle; there is only one person I will put just a little ahead of him, and that is his wife, who has brought up six children. I put the veteran of the great war ahead of every man in the country; but I put ahead even of him the good mother, the mother who has done her duty and brought up well a family of children.

My friends, yesterday I had the pleasure of addressing your

[1] General T. J. Downen, President of the Y.M.C.A., was a Civil War veteran who had lost an arm at Chickamauga.

people in Denver on the subject of Conservation. I noticed that some well-meaning person spoke of the doctrine as the new doctrine of Conservation. It is the identical old doctrine that never has been changed—of Conservation, which means using as fully as possible the resources of the country, but using them in the way that a wise private farmer would use his farm; so that our children shall be better off, and not worse off, because we lived. And I want to call attention to the wonderful work done by the Forest Service in fighting the great forest fires this year. With the very inadequate appropriation made for the Forest Service, nevertheless, that Service, because of the absolute honesty and efficiency with which it has been conducted, has borne itself so as to make an American proud of having such a body of public servants; and they have shown the same qualities of heroism in battling with the fire, at the peril and sometimes to the loss of their lives, that the firemen of the great cities show in dealing with burning buildings.

One word more. I wish I could get down to New Mexico and Arizona, your southern and southwestern neighbors. I raised most of my regiment in what were then the two territories; and you, friends, know that you have a peculiar feeling for the man who has been in the trenches with you. I have been asked by some there to advise them concerning the constitutions of the new states. I do not know enough of the facts to advise them, excepting on this point: Don't let them tie themselves up so that they cannot untie themselves if the need comes. Whenever a new constitution is formed, there are always two sets of people whom you want to watch. In the first place, the demagogue or the well-meaning visionary who wants to realize the millennium by putting what he regards as portions of it in parts of the constitution; and in the next place, the big corporation attorney, who is not after the millennium at all, but who wants to put in, in unobtrusive fashion, something that he thinks of advantage to the special interest which he serves. Now, because of both, and because of the fact that the Convention may adopt the advice of one or the other, let the people insist that when the constitution has been adopted, the people shall be able to amend it as they find its working necessitates. Do not tie up the people so that if they do not like what they have got, they have to keep it anyway. Leave them so that they can make any amendments that are necessary.

Now, friends, you have here a wonderful state; a state of wonderful resources,—agricultural, pastoral, mineral,—a state of farms and ranches, of mines and cities of industry. You have a state with a wonderful industrial future, and a state which also ought to be the playground of America. More and more, our people ought to realize that, for beauty of scenery, they cannot do better than come to Colorado; and as I do not think any eastern man's education complete until he goes west of Missouri, I want to have him come here as much as possible. But though I admire your natural resources, what I really care for is the kind of man, the kind of woman, you have in this state; and I pin my faith to you primarily because I believe in the type of citizenship of your state. I think the average American a pretty good fellow; and I think his wife a still better fellow! And I think that even in states where she does not vote, too! [2] And while I am very glad to see all of you here, those whom I am most glad to see are the men and women who carry small folk. They are sure to be good citizens.

In its essence, good government is nothing very complicated. What we need to insist on is not genius, but the development of the ordinary qualities that make man or woman the kind of man or woman we care to meet in private life. If the man is a good husband, and the woman a good wife; if they do their duty as father and mother; if they are good neighbors, then you have the foundations of citizenship laid. But do not allow any man to impose on you, especially a public man, by asking you to accept decency and domestic virtue as an offset to profligacy in public life. The public man should

[2] While most states still did not permit women to vote on equal terms with men in 1910, Colorado had granted women the suffrage as early as 1893. One member of the Colorado legislature was a woman.

be honest in the biggest and broadest acceptation of the term. If he is not, then it is your fault if you tolerate him in public life, no matter what he may be in private life. Make it felt by your representatives that the taint of corruption ruins a man forever in your eyes. Make it felt that you demand in your representative, not merely law-honesty, not merely the honesty that consists in escaping indictment, but that you demand the honesty that entitles a man to the good will of those who know him intimately enough to tell whether or not he is really straight. And remember that you cannot have honesty in great things unless you have it in small things. If you send to Congress or to the legislature, or put in executive office, a man who will try to blackmail a corporation, you can guarantee that, if the price is high enough, he will sell out to the corporation. Make no mistake; never trust a man who says that he is only a little crooked, and that the crookedness is exercised in your interest. If he will be crooked for you, he will be crooked against you. So I ask that our citizens insist in their public representatives upon the same qualities which they insist upon in private life—upon courage, upon honesty, and upon the saving grace of common sense.

PART THREE

The Word and the Deed

Corruption

Speech before The Hamilton Club, Chicago

8 SEPTEMBER 1910

I have had a long and, to me, a most pleasant and profitable connection with this club.[1] I had known you before I had attained any special prominence in public life. When I came back from the Cuban campaign it was a committee of your club that was practically the first organization to meet me at Montauk Point, and to ask me to come to speak to you; when I was inaugurated as Governor, a body of representatives of this club were present, and at that time you gave me an Abraham Lincoln inkstand, which has stood on my desk ever since, and which is the one I use now; and I think it was this club which was practically the first organization to be so unwise as to formulate a desire to have me made President—

[1] After several months of deadlock, the Illinois legislature on May 13, 1909 chose the Republican, William Lorimer, on the ninety-ninth ballot as the new U.S. Senator from Illinois. Of the 108 votes the "blond boss" of Chicago received, 53 came from Democrats. When the state investigated charges by the *Chicago Tribune* that Lorimer had bought Democratic votes, it uncovered a slush fund of one hundred thousand dollars provided by Chicago corporations to elect Lorimer. Four members of the legislature confessed they had been bribed. The very night Roosevelt spoke, the bribery trial of Lee O'Neill Browne, Democratic leader of the lower house, went to the jury. When Roosevelt came to Chicago, the U.S. Senate was investigating the legality of Lorimer's election to the Senate. Roosevelt created a sensation by refusing to speak at the Hamilton Club if Senator Lorimer, who was to have sat at the speaker's table, was present. The club was forced to withdraw its invitation to Lorimer even though he was a member of the club.

a fact which, whenever any representative body from this club is in New York, I shall do all I can to conceal from the knowledge of Wall Street.

I remember well that at the first dinner of this club which I attended I was brought around by that profound and learned lawyer, the late James Norton, and I remember that the following year he came on to New York to the dinner of the New England Society, I think it was, to speak on behalf of Chicago, and the toastmaster, in introducing him, referred to the fact that Chicago was popularly regarded as having rather a good opinion of itself. And when Mr. Norton got up, he responded that really Chicago had never quite understood why it was not as well entitled to think well of itself as New York was to think well of London.

It was at an address here at the Hamilton Club that I used the expression "strenuous life," an expression which from that day to this I have never more been able to use; and whenever I have come to you, whenever I have spoken either to this club or elsewhere in Chicago, I have always addressed myself to the instant needs of things; for it would not be worth your while to have me come, and it would not be worth my while to come, if I could not speak exactly as I thought upon the questions of the hour. I feel that when I am in Chicago I am in my own city; that I am in one of the centers of the expression of the vital American spirit. Your problems are my problems, for your problems are the problems of the American people.

Now, there are two chief sources of danger to the American people: lawless violence and corruption; lawless violence, which we most often have to face from among the people who have least of the world's goods; and corruption, which we most often have to face from among the people that have most of the world's goods.

The last time I was in Chicago you were engaged in a struggle with the first evil. It was at the time of the great teamsters' strike, that you remember here, and there was some question of the city authorities not being able to deal with it. You were then face to face with an assault by lawless violence upon the foundation of the American government.

I was coming back from the Rocky Mountains at the time, and I had good friends who earnestly advised me to go around Chicago. I decided to go through it, and stopped here. A deputation of the labor men called upon me, and to them I said what I subsequently said at a dinner at which the then Mayor and the then Governor were present, that, vitally interested though I was in all real reforms for the betterment of our people, and eagerly though I desired to help uplift those who were down, and so far as was possible do away with the inequalities of fortune that come from the inequalities of opportunity, yet when there was disorder, when there was lawless violence, all questions of reform had to be postponed until the orderly process of the law was resumed; and that, while I hoped and believed that the municipal authorities themselves would be able to deal with the disorder, yet, if they found it impossible, back of the city stood the state, and back of the state the nation.

I did not hesitate to speak directly then, and just as little shall I hesitate to speak directly now.

In the program to-night you have done me the honor to print certain quotations from speeches I have made, mostly before the Hamilton Club; and the final quotation is: "We must see that there is civic honesty, civic cleanliness, civic good sense, in our whole administration of the city, state, and nation."

My friends, the value of a sentence like that consists exclusively in the way in which we try to live up to it. The worth of what I have to say to you, and whether or not it is worth your while to listen to me, depends upon the way in which we translate words into deeds. It is all right to applaud a sentence like that in favor of civic honesty, stating that civic honesty is essential to the welfare of a nation. It is well enough to applaud it, but woe to you if you applaud the sentence in the abstract and fail to act up to it in the concrete.

It has been well said that the progress, the true progress, of a people can best be gauged by their standard of moral conduct, by their judgment as to what conduct is moral and what conduct is immoral, and by the effectiveness with which they make their approbation of the moral and their disapprobation of the immoral felt. No republic can last if corruption is allowed to eat into its public life. No republic can last if the private citizens sit supinely by and either encourage or tolerate corruption among their representatives.

Each state of the nation, each important city of the Union, has from time to time to face this question. More than once we have been brought face to face with it in the state of New York. You are face to face with it now in the state of Illinois.

I have been reading the reports of the investigations by the two state's attorneys, which resulted in the indictment of four members of the legislature, and together with that I have read the reports of the confession of four other members of the legislature. I was advised to-day by a very worthy friend not to talk on this matter, because it was a "delicate" subject, and he added that no one had been convicted. Now, I feel most strongly that we make the question of public honesty a sham if we limit the use of the word "honesty" to mere law-honesty.

There are big business men whom I have counted as among the most insidious enemies of the real welfare of this republic, although they have been so advised that it would be impossible to convict them, and there have been in the United States, including the state of New York, many public men whose careers have been a scandal throughout the country, although they keep clear of the courts.

Read the confessions of the four men. Read what was developed by the two state's attorneys, one belonging to the one party and one belonging to the other, about the four men against whom they secured indictments, and about other men also. Read that, and I defy any honest man of intelligence not to come to the conclusion that the legislature whose doings have been exposed was guilty of the foulest and basest corruption, and, therefore, of the most infamous treason to American institutions.

Now, I am a good party man, but I am an American first. When we come to questions affecting the vital principles of American life, I know no party. When such a question as corruption is involved, we cannot afford to divide on party lines.

I take just this much account of party in such a case. While I will do my best to get hold of the thief of the opposite party, I will try, if possible, a little harder to get hold of the thief of my own party.

When I was President I endeavored to act so that there should be no need of raising the cry among my opponents of "Turn the rascals out," because I turned them out myself just as fast as I could get at them.

Now, mind you, take my words as worth less than nothing, unless, in looking back, you can see that they were justified by my deeds.

Examine what went on in the Post Office Department, or anywhere else, when corruption was alleged with anything like an offer of proof.

Now, in making these investigations I struck two different sets of cases. There was one set of cases where prosecutions would lie. In those cases I turned the matter over to the Department of Justice. In addition, there was the larger class of cases where there was not sufficient ground for prosecution, but where it was evident that the man was an unfit and an improper public servant; and there I turned him out; and when now and then the man back of him, occasionally belonging to a coordinate branch of the government, would come up and say: "Oh, there is no conviction against him," I said, "No, I dare say that he has practiced law-honesty, but he is a crook, and out he goes."

Now, I could do that with the appointive officers, who held office under me; with the elective officers there is but one body that can do that, and that is the people. It depends upon you, upon the people of America, whether you will permit a man to represent you because he has been acquitted in a court of law, or because there has been a mistrial, so that enough jurors have believed in him to get him off,—whether you will permit that man to represent you, or whether you will take the stand that where you have evidence of a kind which may not be legal, but which convinces every honest man of intelligence, you will not submit to the pollution of American life by putting such a man in high official position.

Now, in each nation, in every form of government, there are base flatterers. The same individual who in a monarchy would be a courtier and flatter the king, in a republic turns demagogue and flatters those whom he thinks will cast the most votes. They are of just the same type. The one is just as bad as the other; the only difference is that they are functioning under different conditions. It is a favorite—I won't say argument—but a favorite assertion of men of that type when some public servant has been found guilty of conduct that should disgrace him to say, "We will go to the people for his vindication; we will see if we can't secure him an election." Sometimes they succeed. A great many thoroughly good people, thoroughly good citizens, have no special means of information, are ignorant of what really has happened, and may on occasions like that be misled; but if they are misled, and if they do, so far as in them lies, attempt to vindicate a dishonest and unfaithful public servant by electing him, they don't vindicate him, they merely disgrace themselves and us.

I call the attention of the people who make that argument to this fact: We produced in New York once an arch scoundrel whose fame became international,—Boss Tweed,—and after Tweed was convicted he was elected to the state senate as a "vindication." Has that made any difference in the judgment passed upon Tweed's honesty by history? Not a bit, but it shed an unfortunate light upon the standards of some of the citizens of New York at that time. They did not help Tweed. They did not help his reputation. They hurt themselves, and they hurt the entire American body politic, for none of us can commit such a folly without having the effect felt both by ourselves and by others.

If because a postmaster who had been guilty of crooked transactions could not have been convicted in a court of law I had permitted him to continue in office, I would not have made that man's character good; I would merely have shown that mine was bad; and the same thing applies to the body politic.

In other forms of government than ours there may be a certain kind of progress even if the average man is not what he should be; but in our government, in a great democracy like ours, the stream cannot rise higher than its source. You cannot have honesty in public life unless the average citizen demands honesty in public life.

If the people of America are content to send to represent them in the state or the national legislature men who they know in their heart of hearts have not obtained their offices honestly, but have obtained their offices dishonestly and by corruption, who they know have practiced corruption in public life, they may make up their minds that they will get the government to which they are entitled, and a bad government it will be.

Now, my friends, I do not suppose that if we decline to be honest and to insist on honesty in public life for our own sakes, we can be expected to do so for the sake of others; and yet, in addition to making the appeal for honesty to you and to the citizens of Illinois, for the sake of Illinois, and for the sake of America, I make the appeal also for the sake of the world.

Last spring, in Europe, there were two things that struck me especially as I talked with the average man. The first was that the man looked toward America as the land of golden hope, as the land of a partially realized ideal, as a land where it was really being shown that the people could govern themselves justly and righteously and in their own interest.

And the second thing was that that faith in America was continually being shaken by stories that reached them of corruption in American business and in American public life. Every act of corruption here, every gross scandal, every bit of flagrant dishonesty in big business or in politics, or in connection with the complex web that weaves together strands of big business and strands of politics—every such instance, when carried abroad, brings sneering satisfaction to the heart of every reactionary, who is glad to say: "Yes, that is what comes of democracy. That is what you get when the people try to govern themselves. It shows that they cannot govern themselves." And every such instance dims the hope of the poor and the oppressed who strive to believe and haltingly do believe that here, somehow or other, we have arranged a condition of things in which the injustices of the world elsewhere are at least partially remedied.

My friends, I ask you men of Illinois that you purify your politics, that you hold accountable the scoundrel, great or small, who has been guilty of corruption, that you insist on cleanliness in your public life; and I ask it in your name and for your sakes; I ask it for the sake of the American people; and I ask it for the sake of all the nations of the world, that their hope may not be made dim, and that they may continue to cherish the ideal of the possibility of having a government of, by, and for the people, that shall mean also a government of justice and a government of honesty.

Law, Order, and Justice

Speech at Columbus
10 SEPTEMBER 1910

Ever since I have been in Ohio I have been hearing of the lamentable conditions here in Columbus due to the street railway strike.[1] Both sides have written to me stating the case as they saw it, and each side urged me to come. While I freely say that I did not like to come, I like still less to dodge.

As I had started to say,[2] I find that my speech was put down as being a speech upon law and order. I have asked that it be changed—that it be put down as a speech upon law, order, and justice.

The first essential to the achievement of justice is that law and order shall obtain, that violence shall be repressed, that the orderly course of law shall be unobstructed, and that those who

---

[1] Columbus had been torn by a violent streetcar strike. Workers had engaged in an armed battle with railway detectives and strikebreakers. Dynamite had been placed on the tracks; one car had been blown up; and mobs had wrecked cars. Strikers had beaten up crews and shot at passing streetcars. Passengers had been wounded by flying missiles. Roosevelt spoke at Goodale Park guarded by an escort of regular troops. A week later, Roosevelt claimed for his Columbus speech: "I made an address filled with platitudes of the most direct ad hominem type, pointing at the leaders of the strike and their counsel, who were but thirty feet away from me; and my platitudes resulted in the restoration of order and the stoppage of violence within twenty-four hours." (This was a typically Rooseveltian view of events; by the time he arrived in Columbus, the tide against violence had already turned.)

[2] Roosevelt began his speech in the midst of such disorder that few heard his opening sentences.

commit violence shall be sternly punished. But while this is the first vital essential towards the achievement of justice, it is of value primarily as leading up to justice. After law and order have been obtained,—not before, after,—then comes the question of seeing that absolute justice is done.

I am not competent to speak as to the exact facts, or in detail, of your trouble here. I have received from reputable men conflicting allegations as to what has occurred;[3] so that all I can do is to set forth certain general principles which apply here as they apply in all similar cases.

In the first place, there must be obedience to the law; there must be a cessation of violence and bad conduct. It is admitted by almost everyone that there have been repeated and brutal acts of violence, ranging from actual assault to bomb-throwing, and, finally, to the use of that weapon of the meanest, the basest, and the most cowardly type of assassin—dynamite. There is not much to choose among assassins; but the assassin who tries to kill a man, or men, with dynamite and himself escape all personal risk occupies an evil eminence on the table-land of infamy. Now, the first requisite is to establish order; and the first duty of every official, in state and city alike, high and low, is to see that order obtains and that violence is definitely stopped. One of the things of which I am proud is my connection with the New York police force. I have the greatest regard for the policeman who does his duty. I put him high among the props of the state; but the policeman who mutinies, or refuses to perform his duty, stands on a level lower than that of the professional lawbreaker.[4] Such a policeman ranks with the soldier who mutinies in the face of the enemy, and should be consigned to the same pit of oblivion. I ask, then, not only that civic officials perform their duties, but that you, the people, insist upon their performing

[3] As he headed west two weeks before, both sides had presented their cases to him, and, since then, he had been receiving communications about the strike.
[4] Thirty-two Columbus policemen had mutinied and refused to do police duty in the strike. Several policemen on duty about the speaker's stand joined warmly in the applause that followed Roosevelt's sentence condemning the mutineers.

them. You are not to be excused if you fail to demand that your representatives perform the first duty of civilized people by seeing that violence is stopped and that the laws are obeyed.

I ask this particularly of the wage workers, and employees, and men on strike. It is to the interest of everybody that law and order shall prevail; but it is specially to their interest because the question of the rights and wrongs of the controversy cannot be settled as they should be settled until there is order, until the law is observed. I ask them, not merely passively, but actively, to help in restoring order. I ask them to clear their skirts of all suspicion of sympathizing with disorder, and, above all, the suspicion of sympathizing with those who commit brutal and cowardly assaults.

If it be true—I don't know whether it is true or not—but if it is, as alleged to me—if it be true that the attorneys of the strikers habitually appear for every miscreant who is arrested for assaulting cars, for assaulting other people, and furnish them bail bonds, then, in their own interest and for their good name, let the wage workers get rid of the attorneys.[5] Let them get rid of the attorney who by such action inevitably tends to cast a doubt upon the sincerity of the expressions of the men who disclaim sympathy with those outrages.

And, now, what I have said of the laboring men applies just as much to the capitalists and the capitalists' representatives. A year ago, Judge Sater[6] sat in southern Ohio on a case brought before him affecting the striking miners. An injunction was asked for against the miners. He declined to give it, and read to both parties from the bench a lecture to which, for their good fortune, they paid heed. He told the miners that their worst foes were among themselves, among those members and sympathizers who committed acts of violence; and he told the employers that if they, by their hired men

[5] This sentence was interpreted as a slap at one of the labor attorneys, Frank S. Monnett, who was running for Congress in Columbus on the Democratic ticket. The former Attorney General of Ohio, Monnett had been William Randolph Hearst's attorney and had won fame by prosecuting Standard Oil.

[6] John Elbert Sater (1854-1937), U.S. district judge for the Southern District of Ohio from 1907 to 1924.

and representatives, committed acts of violence, they, in their turn, occupied the same disgraceful position that their opponents occupied; that the law was the same for both, and justice and good conduct were demanded alike of each party to the controversy.

In all great labor struggles, not only are the capitalists and the employees parties in interest, but there is another party, and that third party is the people as a whole. You here are the party in interest, and peculiarly so in a controversy like the present, where a public service corporation is involved which has a peculiar and special connection with the government and with the people.

Now, then, your first duty is, as I have said, to see that law and order obtain. It is the duty of your representatives in public life to demand it of the lawbreaker, not as a favor, but as a right, which you will punish him for failing to fulfill; and it is to the interest of all of you to demand it, but, most of all, it is the interest of the wage workers. But your duty does not stop there. It has only just begun. There can be no justice without law and order; but law and order are well-nigh valueless unless used as a foundation upon which justice is built up as a super-structure.

As I have said to you, conflicting statements have been made to me as to the original cause of the trouble. It has been alleged to me by reputable men that originally the trouble began because of the discharge of certain men who asked for an increase in wages. It has been alleged to me that the struggle has been continued because of the open or covert determination of the employers not to permit a union to exist among their employees. Both allegations have been denied, and I have no facts before me which enable me to decide whether or not they are correct.

As to the first allegation, it would be an act so infamous to discharge a man because he asked for an increase in wages, that I can hardly believe it can have occurred. But it would be almost as bad to discharge a man because he belonged to, or was preparing to enter, or organize, a union. I am an honorary member of a union myself. If I were a wage worker, I should certainly join a union; but when

I was in I would remember that I was first of all an American citizen. Uncle Sam comes on top in everything. I would certainly join a union. In our modern industrial system the union is just as necessary as the corporation, and in the modern field of industrialism it is often an absolute necessity that there should be collective bargaining by the employees with the employers; and such collective bargaining is but one of the many benefits conferred by wisely and honestly organized unions that act properly. Of course, it is outrageous to force a man to join a union, just as it is outrageous to take part in, or encourage, the so-called secondary boycott; but it is no less an outrage to discriminate against him because he wishes to have a union, or to refuse to deal with a union when organized. The union has the same right to exist that the corporation has, and it is unfair to refuse to deal with it as it is to refuse to deal with the corporation. Show your willingness to give the union its full rights, and you will be stronger when you set your faces like flint, as I have set mine, against the union when it is wrong. So that as soon as law and order have been obtained, it becomes your duty, you, the people, through your municipal or through your state authorities, to insist upon a thorough investigation by competent and disinterested authorities who will put before us an authoritative statement of the rights and wrongs of both sides; and then demand a thoroughgoing remedy for any wrong.

A case like this should be always a matter for mediation or arbitration. If such is refused by either party, shape your laws so that mediation and arbitration can be secured. If you need to have a constitutional amendment for your purpose, amend the constitution; but don't wait for the amendment to see substantial justice done in this case. See to it.

I have got but two minutes more. I have not spoken long; but you will admit I have spoken to the point. See to it that you find out the facts and find out what the corporation has done. If it has acted properly, decide in its favor; if it has not, decide against it. If there has been injustice done, see that the injustice is remedied.

See that the public service corporation acts for the service of the people. If the municipal and the state authorities mean business they can make the corporation do what is right. See that the evil is remedied, and that you are guaranteed against a repetition of the evil. In short, my friends, I can sum it up in this way: You, the people here, have two duties in this crisis. You have to face the need of exercising two prime duties of American citizenship—insistence upon law and order, and the use of that insistence as a stepping-stone for obtaining justice. Law and order first.

To-morrow is Sunday; to-morrow is a time when you may be threatened with disorder. The wage workers and the representatives of the companies should make it evident that they wish the law absolutely obeyed; that there is no chance of saying that either the labor organizations or the corporation favors lawbreakers or lawbreaking. But let your public servants trust, not in the good will of either side, but to the might of the civil arm, and see that law rules, that order obtains, and that every miscreant, every scoundrel who seeks brutally to assault any other man—whatever that other man's status—is punished with the utmost severity. Keep order now. Frown on disorder and violence now, and put them down with ruthless severity; and then, friends, when you have obtained law and order, remember that it is useless to have obtained them unless upon them you build a superstructure of justice. After finding out the facts, see that justice is done; see that injustice that has been perpetrated in the past is remedied, and see that the chance of doing injustice in the future is minimized. Take these two positions, and you will have deserved well, not only of the city of Columbus, not only of the state of Ohio, but of the people of the great republic in which we are living and in whose citizenship we exult without measure.

PART FOUR

The New Nationalism
and
The Old Moralities

The New Nationalism and the Old Moralities

Speech at Syracuse
17 SEPTEMBER 1910

Criticism has been made of certain of my speeches in the West where I advocated what has been called the "New Nationalism." [1] But the New Nationalism really means nothing but an application to new conditions of certain old and fundamental moralities. It means an invitation to meet the new problems of the present day in precisely the spirit in which Lincoln and the men of his day met their new problems. In my western speeches I said chiefly what I again and again said in messages to Congress when I was President. I very slightly developed the doctrines contained in these presidential addresses in order to meet the development of the new conditions; and the chief way in which I developed them was to include a quotation from Abraham Lincoln and construe it in connection with the very old doctrine of eminent domain.

Now what I say in the West I of course say here. Whether it is sound or not can, I think, be determined by the simple expedient of asking whether any party is willing frankly to take the other side of the propositions of which complaint is made. If so, it would be a good thing to have the issue made in clean-cut fashion

[1] The Republican Party in New York was controlled by the Old Guard. Syracuse was one of the centers of opposition to the doctrines of the "New Nationalism."

before the people; for in the end the people would most certainly decide in favor of the principles embodied in the New Nationalism, because otherwise this country could not continue to be a true republic, a true democracy.

Take, for instance, what I said in reference to two decisions of the Supreme Court. It was in the course of an address in which I dwelt upon the great need of having the spheres of activity of the national and state governments extended to cover the whole field of our life that can properly be touched by legislation at all, so that there shall not be left a debatable land in which neither nation nor state has real power, and which can serve as a place of refuge for men who wish to escape all effective control under the law, and especially for the great corporations which wish thus to escape control. One decision was in the Knight Sugar case, in which, according to the dissenting opinion of Justice Harlan, the judgment of the court placed the public "so far as national power is concerned [the only power which could be effective] entirely at the mercy of combinations which arbitrarily control the prices of articles purchased to be transported from one state to another state." I merely took the view which the learned justice had thus taken in his dissenting opinion. It is, in my judgment, unquestionably the correct view. The decision has been a bar in the path of those who are honestly endeavoring to secure adequate control over great corporations doing an interstate business. Those who criticize me are also criticizing a justice of the Supreme Court, Mr. Harlan. Do my critics take the position that the people shall not be able to control the management and activities of these great monopolistic corporations doing an interstate business? If so, let them frankly avow their position. If not, let them cease their criticism.

The second decision was one against state's rights, prohibiting the state of New York to regulate in very moderate fashion the hours of work in bakery and confectionery establishments where the conditions are such that excessive hours of labor continued day in and day out may endanger the health and shorten the lives of the workingmen. Here what I said was based upon the dissenting opinions of Justices Harlan, White, Day, and Holmes, who specifically upheld the view that the state had the power to regulate the hours of labor under such conditions, taking the broad ground that "it is the primary duty of the state to guard and protect the health and safety of its people." Here I held that the dissenting justices were right in their views, and that, however honest men may be who revive the long outworn doctrine that the state shall not interfere with the "liberty" of laborers who are driven by grinding need to contract to work for an excessive number of hours under unhealthy conditions, yet such doctrine is essentially anti-social, and is really a relic of a past geological age in our social and economic history. If my opponents disagree with me, let them frankly say that the state has no right to limit the hours of labor of men employed under conditions dangerous to their health and welfare. If they do so, I take issue with them. If they do not, then they have no right to criticize what I have said.

Fifty-three years ago Abraham Lincoln was assailed for his repeated criticisms of the Supreme Court in the Dred Scott case. As regards this decision he announced, not once, but again and again, that he held it to be not merely the right but the duty of citizens, who felt that judicial decisions were erroneous and damaging, loyally to abide by the decisions as long as they stood, but to try hard to secure their reversal; his language on one occasion being as follows:—

"We do not propose in any violent way [to] disturb the rights of property thus settled. . . . We propose so resisting it [the decision] as to have it reversed if we can, and a new judicial rule established upon this subject."

He repeated this statement in slightly differing language in speech after speech.

Moreover, he used very strong language about the decision, far stronger than I should dream of using, or than it would be proper to use, about the decisions with which I now deal. But his view as to his right and duty to call attention to an erroneous decision which vitally affected the rights of the people was, I think, entirely sound. At any rate, if I have erred in commenting as I have commented upon the decisions in question, I err in company with Abraham Lincoln.

The criticism of me is perhaps well summed up in the following speech of an eminent public man:—

"He makes war on the decision of the Supreme Court. I wish to say to you, fellow citizens, that I have no war to make on that decision, or any other ever rendered by the Supreme Court. I am content to take that decision as it stands delivered by the highest judicial tribunal on earth, a tribunal established by the Constitution of the United States for that purpose, and hence that decision becomes the law of the land, binding on you, on me, and on every other good citizen, whether we like it or not. Hence, I do not choose to go into argument to prove, before this audience, whether or not he [the Chief Justice] understood the law better than Theodore Roosevelt."

Now, gentleman, I have made one change in the above quotation. The last words were not "Theodore Roosevelt," the last words were "Abraham Lincoln," and this attack, made nearly fifty-three years ago upon Abraham Lincoln, is precisely and exactly the kind of attack made upon me at the moment. Abraham Lincoln felt and professed, throughout his life, the same profound respect for the Supreme Court that, of course, I feel, and that I have again and again in public speech and messages, as President of the United States, expressed. An upright judge is a higher and better public servant than any other man can possibly be, and it is a cause of pride to every American citizen that our Supreme Court is the most influential judicial tribunal in the entire world. I have quoted Abraham Lincoln; let me quote him again: "We believe in obedience to and respect for the judicial department of government. We think its decisions on constitutional questions when fully settled should control." I agree absolutely with this sentence of

Abraham Lincoln, not the less because I also believe in what Lincoln said immediately afterwards: "But we think this decision erroneous, and we shall do what we can to have it overruled."

Nor do I have to go only to the statesmen of the past for precedents. The President of the United States, Mr. Taft has served his country honorably and uprightly in many positions,—as judge, as Governor of the Philippines, as Secretary of War, and now as President,—for to him and the Congress acting with him, we owe the creation of a Tariff Commission, the adoption of maximum and minimum tariff law treaties with foreign powers, the proper treatment of the Philippines under the tariff, the increase in the efficiency of the Interstate Commerce Law, the beginning of a national legislative program providing for the exercise of the taxing power in connection with corporations doing an interstate business, a Postal Savings Bank Bill, the constitution of a commission to report a remedy for overcapitalization in connection with the issue of stocks and bonds; but few of his services are more deserving of record that what he said in this very matter of criticism of the judiciary. Speaking as a United States circuit judge, fifteen years ago, he said: "The opportunity freely and publicly to criticize judicial action is of vastly more importance to the body politic than the immunity of courts and judges from unjust aspersions and attack. Nothing tends more to render judges careful in their decisions and anxiously solicitous to do exact justice than the consciousness that every act of theirs is to be submitted to the intelligent scrutiny and candid criticism of their fellow men. In the case of judges having a life tenure, indeed, their very independence makes the right freely to comment on their decisions of greater importance, because it is the only practicable and available instrument in the hands of a free people to keep such judges alive to the reasonable demands of those they serve."

We who work for the New Nationalism are not working in any spirit of mere faction or party. We recognize parties as necessary instruments for government under popular conditions, just as we recognize corporations as necessary instruments in modern business, and just as we recognize unions as necessary instruments in the elevation of wage workers under modern industrial conditions. But we believe that true loyalty to a party consists chiefly in making that party the efficient servant of the whole people.

Among those who manage our government, state and national, in legislative and in judicial positions, we regard the one vital and essential matter to be honesty. The crook in public life is the gravest menace to our political institutions, and we call on all good citizens to drive him out of public life. Whether his crookedness takes the form of blackmail or of bribery—we care nothing whether he receive the bribe or give it—is of small consequence. In any event he is a traitor to democracy and a foe to republican institutions; and against him we war without mercy; and we will reject without hesitation any plea advanced on his behalf, no matter what may be the influence, political, social, or commercial, that stands behind him.

We believe in the hearty encouragement and reward of individual excellence, but we believe also in steadily using the power of the government to secure economic democracy as well as political democracy. Our ideal is to secure, so far as by law it is possible to secure, a reasonable approximation to equality of opportunity for all men, so that (as far as it is humanly possible to secure it) each man shall have the chance to start fair in the race of life and to show the stuff that is in him, unhelped by special privilege for himself and unhampered by special privilege for others. We know that an ideal like this can never be entirely realized, but we believe it our duty to do whatever is possible to bring about a measurable approximation to this ideal. We entirely understand that after the best possible laws have been obtained, and after they have been enforced in the most efficient possible manner, it will yet remain true that the chief factor in each man's success or failure must be that man's individual character; but while fully recognizing this fact, we nevertheless insist that good laws and honest administration of these laws can be made to play a very real and effective part in the betterment of mankind. According to our ability we intend to safeguard the rights of the mighty; but we intend no less jealously to safeguard the rights of the lowly. Our ideal is equal justice for all; justice alike for the rich man and the poor man who do right; and the same stern justice for the rich man and the poor man who do wrong.

We cordially believe in the rights of property. We think that normally and in the long run the rights of humanity, the rights of mankind, coincide with the rights of property, and that the two sets of rights are in large part inextricably interwoven; and so we would protect property in all its rights. But we feel that if in exceptional cases there is any conflict between the rights of property and the rights of man, then we must stand for the rights of man. And we believe that where property has accumulated in such masses that it becomes heaped-up wealth, fairly fabulous in its extent and power, then there arises a real reason not merely for safeguarding the rights of wealth but for safeguarding the people against the wrongs and abuses of wealth, and especially of wealth in its corporate capacity, of wealth functioning as corporate capital. The great captains of industry do well and are entitled to great rewards only in so far as they render great service; they are invaluable as long as they in good faith act as efficient servants of the public; they become intolerable when they behave as the masters of the public. The corporation is the creature of the people; and it must not be allowed to become the ruler of the people.

Politically we believe that the people should act with justice and moderation, and that it is eminently necessary that they should show self-control. But we also believe that this should be literally self-control and not control by outsiders; that they should be controlled by themselves and not by political bosses, or by the direct or indirect use of wealth, and least of all by a combination between political bossism and big business. People are apt to say that bossism is merely another term for leadership. I do not think that this is so. Of course there are all degrees in bossism; and of course the mere fact that a man is a boss does not in the least justify the kind of attack upon him that ought to be made upon a corrupt and unfaithful public servant. Nevertheless, we think that the boss is a bad development in our politics. It is necessary and desirable that there should be leaders, but it is unnecessary and undesirable that there should be bosses. The leader leads the people; the boss drives the people. The leader gets his hold by open appeal to the reason and conscience of his followers; the boss keeps his hold by manipulation, by intrigue, by secret and furtive appeals to many forms of self-interest, and sometimes to very base forms of self-interest. The leader wars on the crook and seeks to drive him from power; the boss too often protects the crook and seeks to profit by his existence. The leader treats the unfaithful public servant as the worst foe of the party to which he nominally belongs, and refuses entirely to recognize him as a party representative; the boss too often uses and shields him. Leadership is carried on in the open light of day; bossism derives its main strength from what is done under cover of darkness.

Of course leadership must not only be brave and honest, but it must be sober and must accord with the dictates of common sense. Exactly as the conservative who favors abuses and connives at corruption is in reality the worst enemy of conservatism, so the popular leader or reformer who acts in the spirit of the demagogue, or of the wild-eyed visionary, who incites to excess and to rash action and stirs up class hatred, is himself the worst foe of progress, the most dangerous enemy of the popular cause which he professes to champion. There must be progress; a great democracy which ceases to be progressive soon also ceases to be either great or democratic; but the progress must be wise, sober, moderate, if it is to be permanent. If we attempt merely to stand still, we are certain to go backward. If under the theory that we are making progress we go in the wrong direction, we shall have to waste much time in retracing our steps. But progress there must and shall be. The past century has been one of gigantic material prosperity, of gigantic accumulation of prosperity. Our task is to preserve that prosperity, in the interest of all of us; but it is also in the interest of all of us to work for a less unequal division of the prosperity. We believe in material well-being as absolutely essential. It is only upon a foundation of material well-being that the greatness of a nation can be built. But the foundation is in no way sufficient in itself. Material well-being is a great good, but it is a great good chiefly as a means for the upbuilding upon it of a high and fine type of character, private and public. Upon our national wellbeing as a foundation we must upbuild the structure of a lofty national life, raised in accordance with the doctrine that "righteousness exalteth a nation."